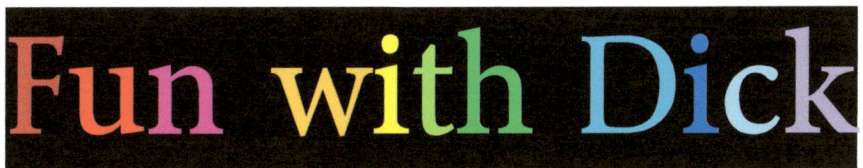

Fun with Dick

Photos: **Franz Josef**

Cover Design: **Jason Roberts**

I0483352

Copyright 2009

First Collector's Edition: Limited to 1000 copies

Available at: Amazon.com

For special discounts on quantity orders for resale, fund raising or sales promotion contact: humanpotentialpress@yahoo.com

All about Dick

Suitable for mounting or framing, these photos of Dick were created by Franz Josef. All are in camera compositions – no manipulation. "A single portrait of Dick can take several weeks to perfect," said Mr. Josef. "Finding clothes and accessories small enough to fit Dick is time consuming. Doll sections in toy departments are my favorite hunting grounds. But explaining to mall security that I have to remove the doll's clothes to see if they fit Dick is very embarrassing. However, they are usually very kind and treat me to free coffee, donuts and an occasional psychiatric evaluation."

Mr. Josef has over 350 photo puns in his private public pun portfolio. The first public exhibition of his Dick collection was at Nude Nite, a juried art event in central Florida. Regarding his first public exposure he commented, "I work hard and take my work very seriously. I was puzzled by the side splitting laughter it received."

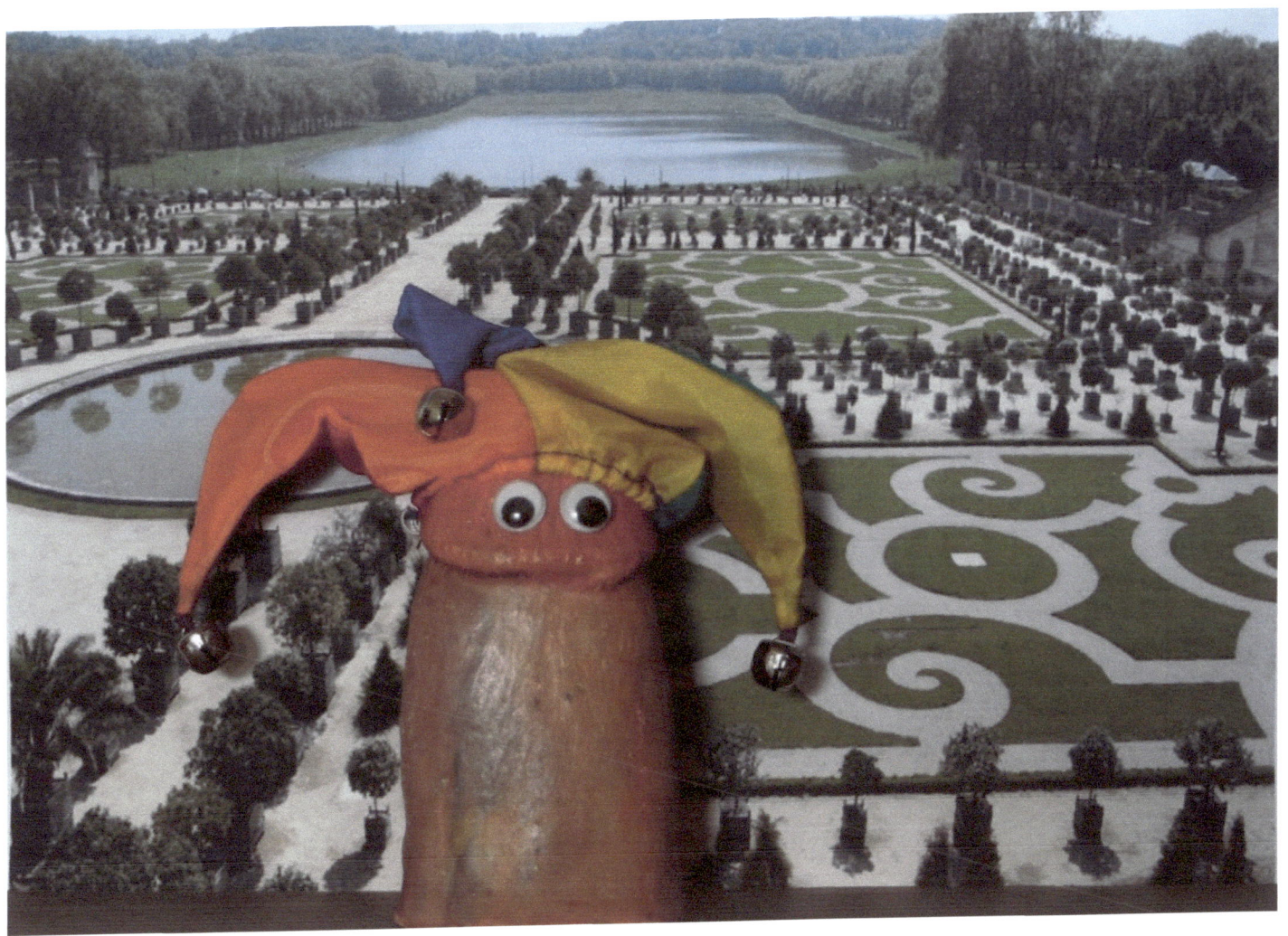

JESTER

PEACOCK

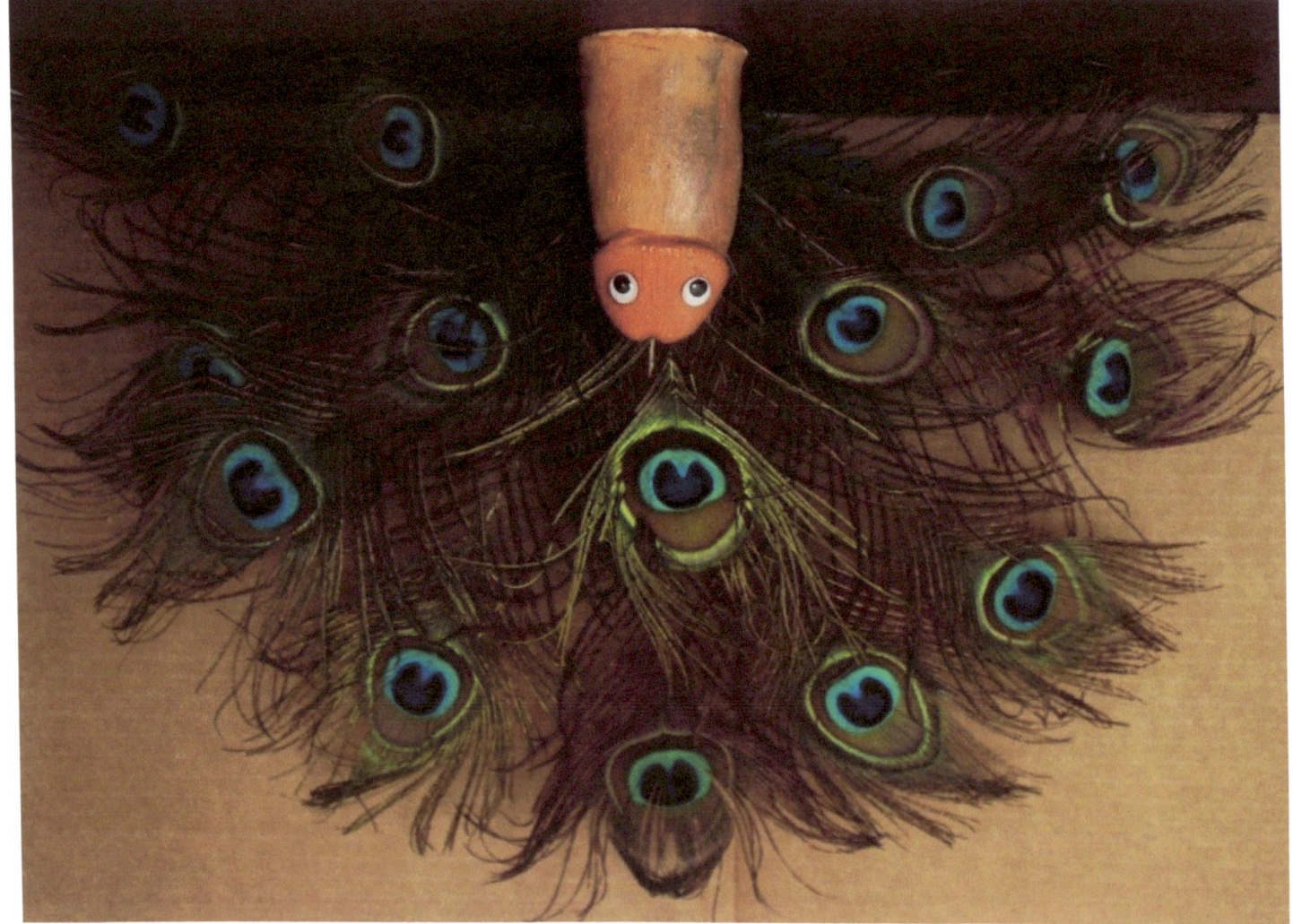

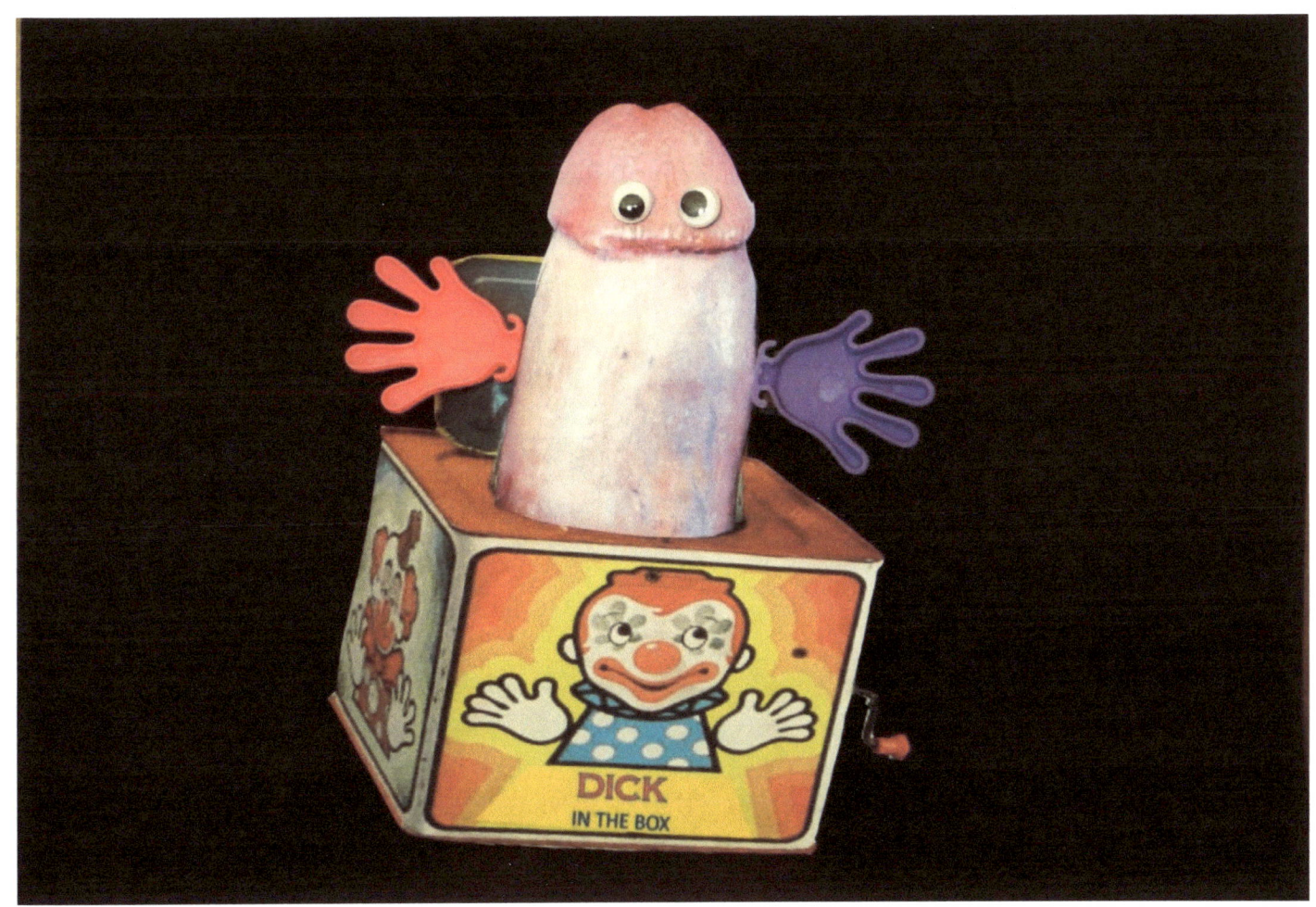

DICK IN THE BOX

PRICKUPINE

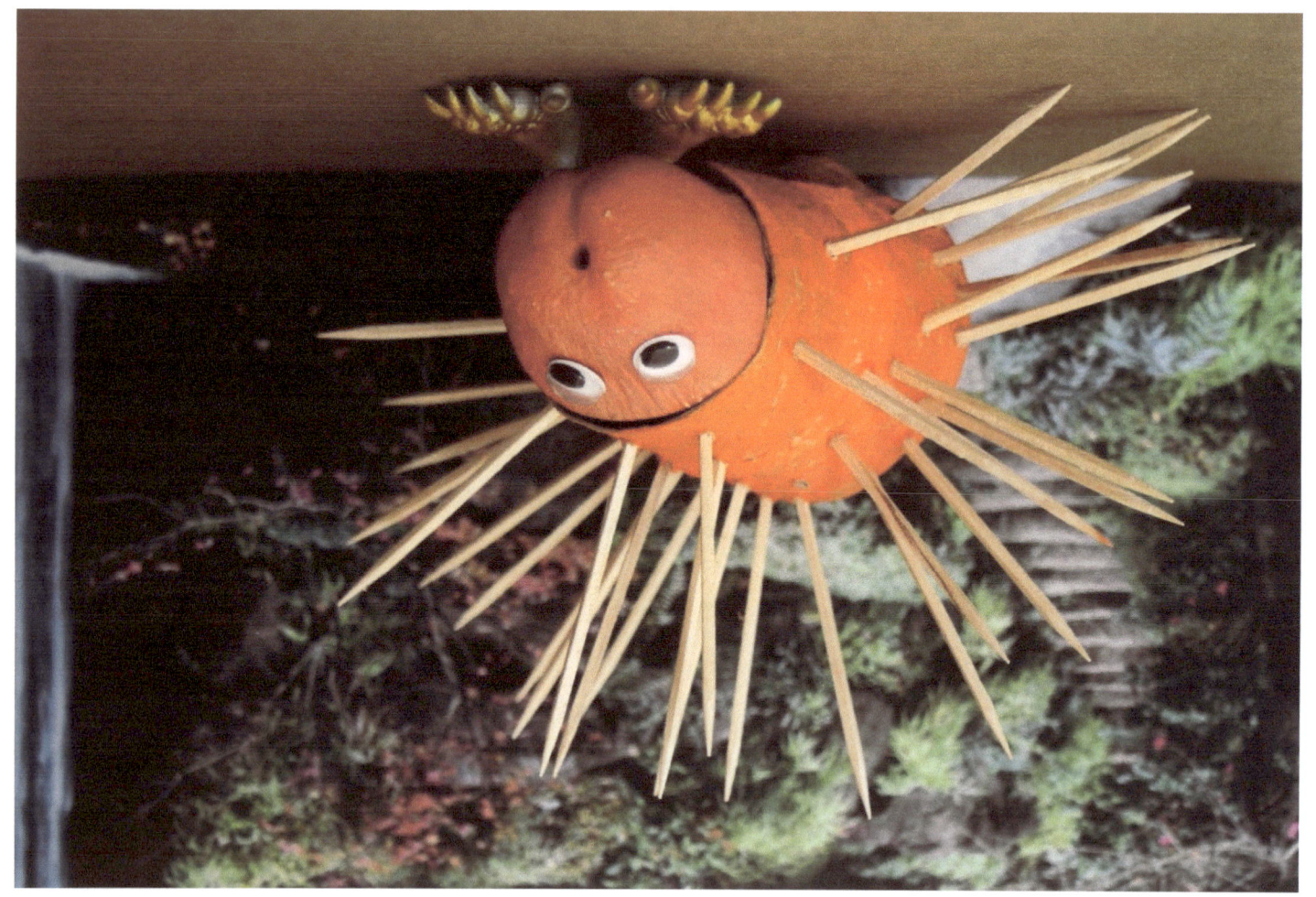

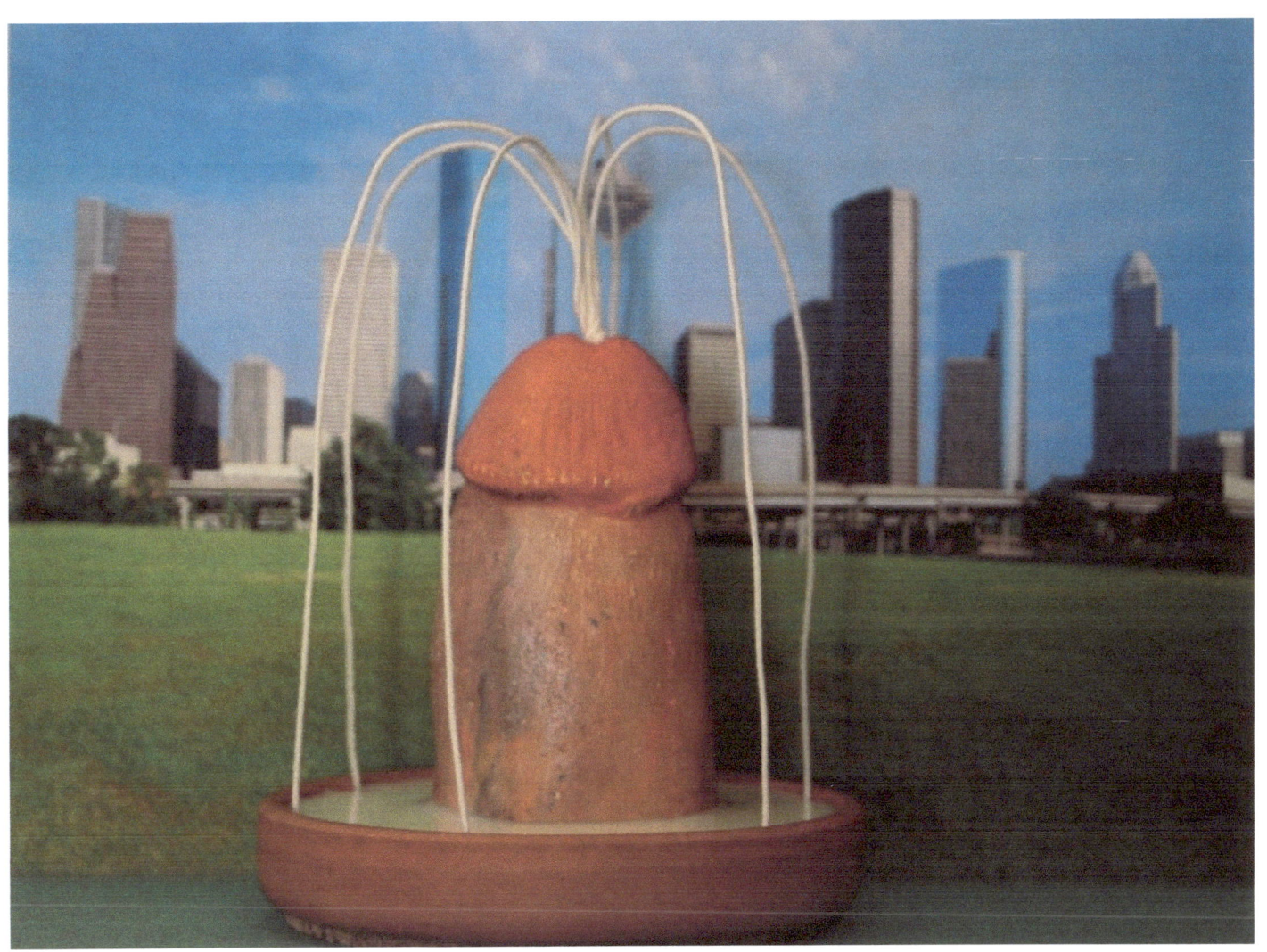

FOUNTAIN OF YOUTH

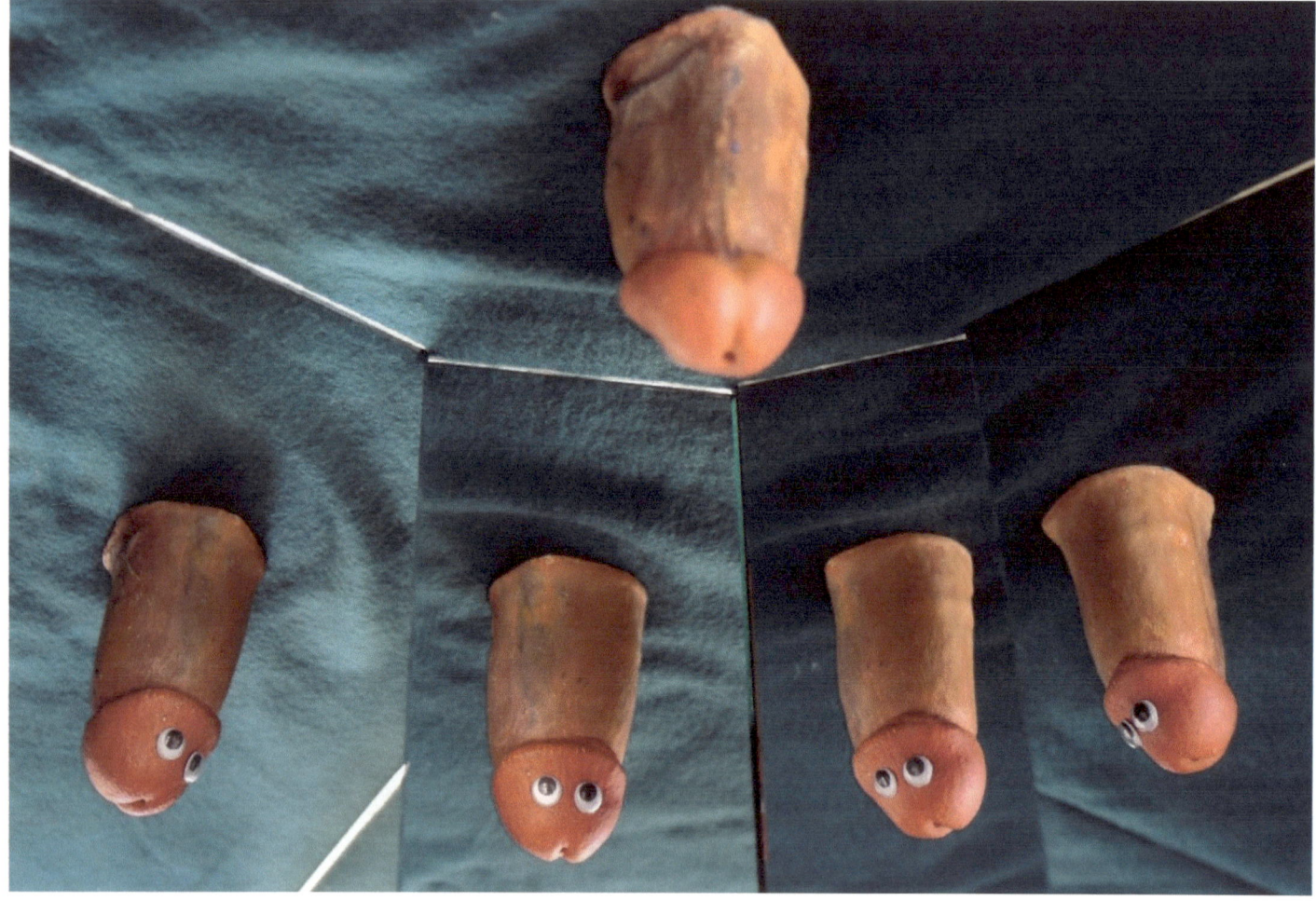

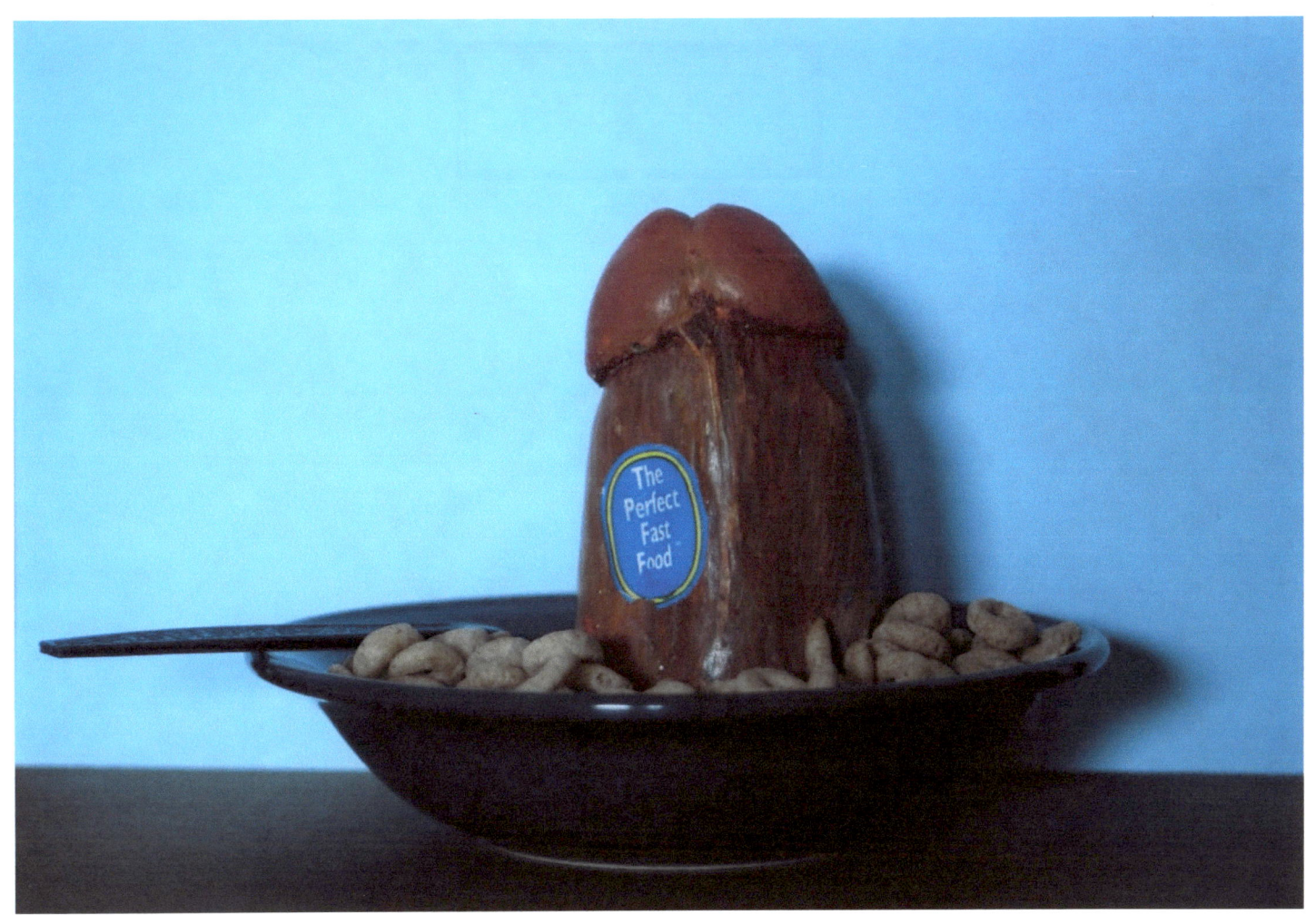

The Perfect Fast Food

BREAKFAST OF CHAMPIONS

DICKTATOR

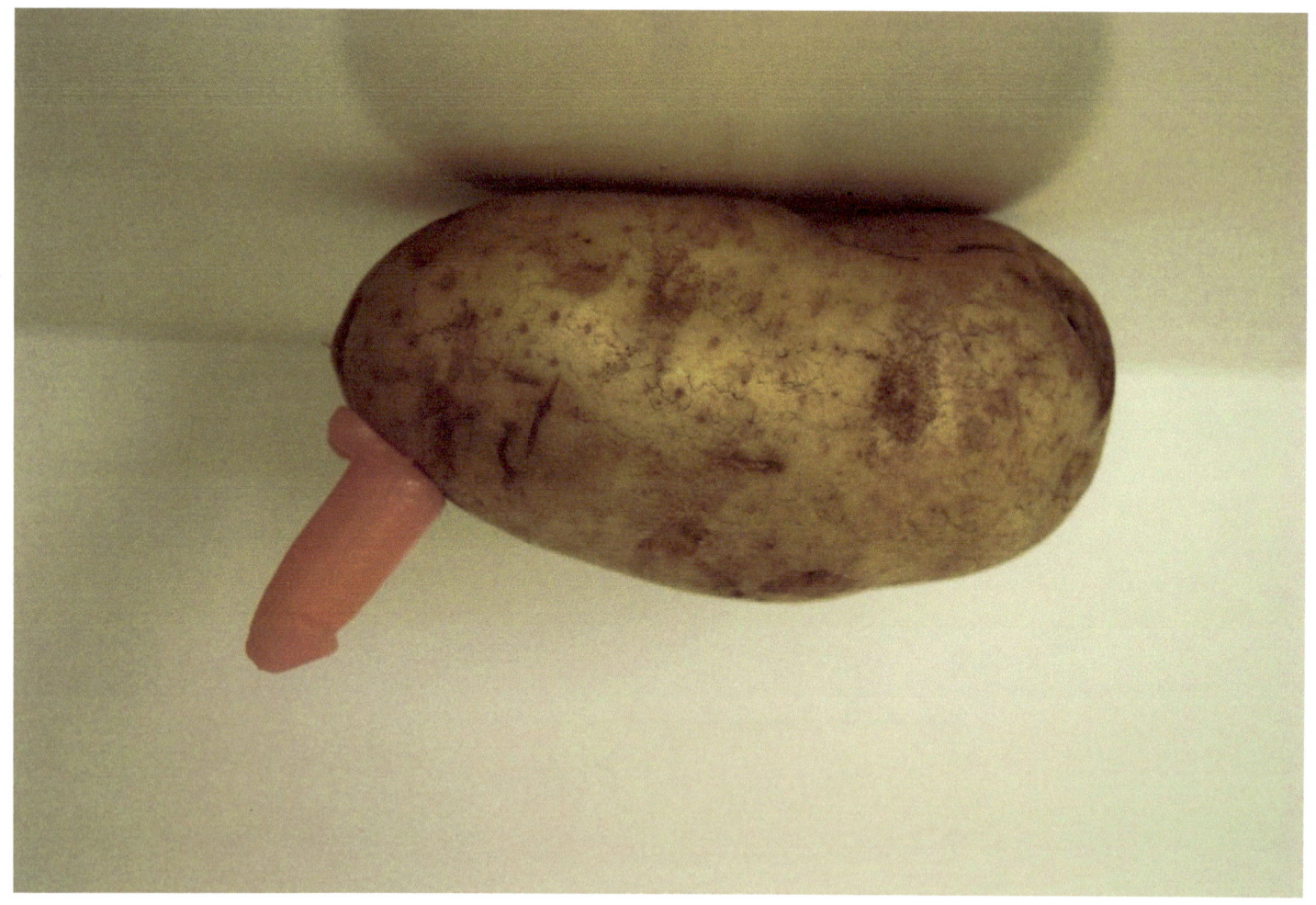

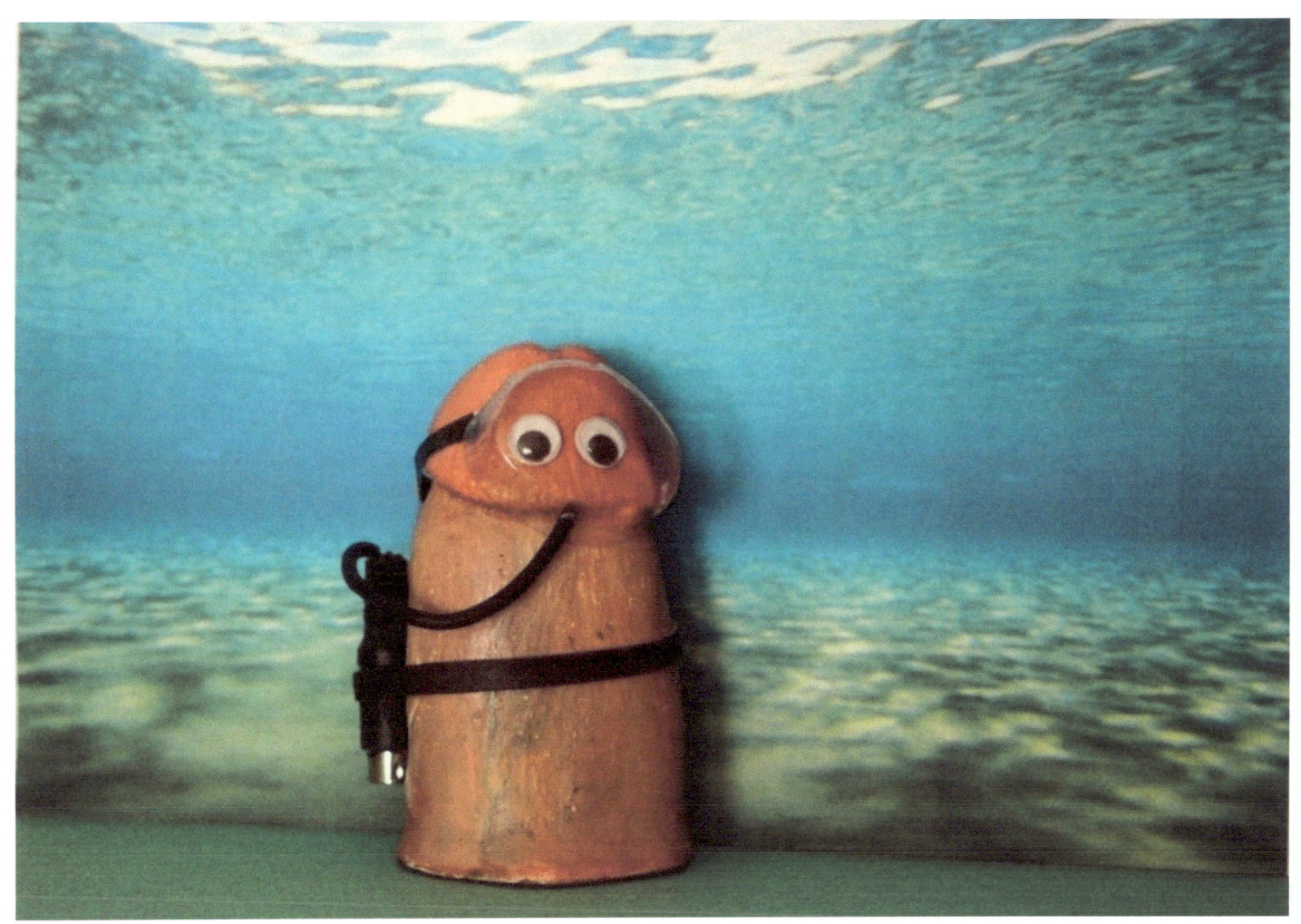

MUFF DIVER

STEROID OVERDOSE

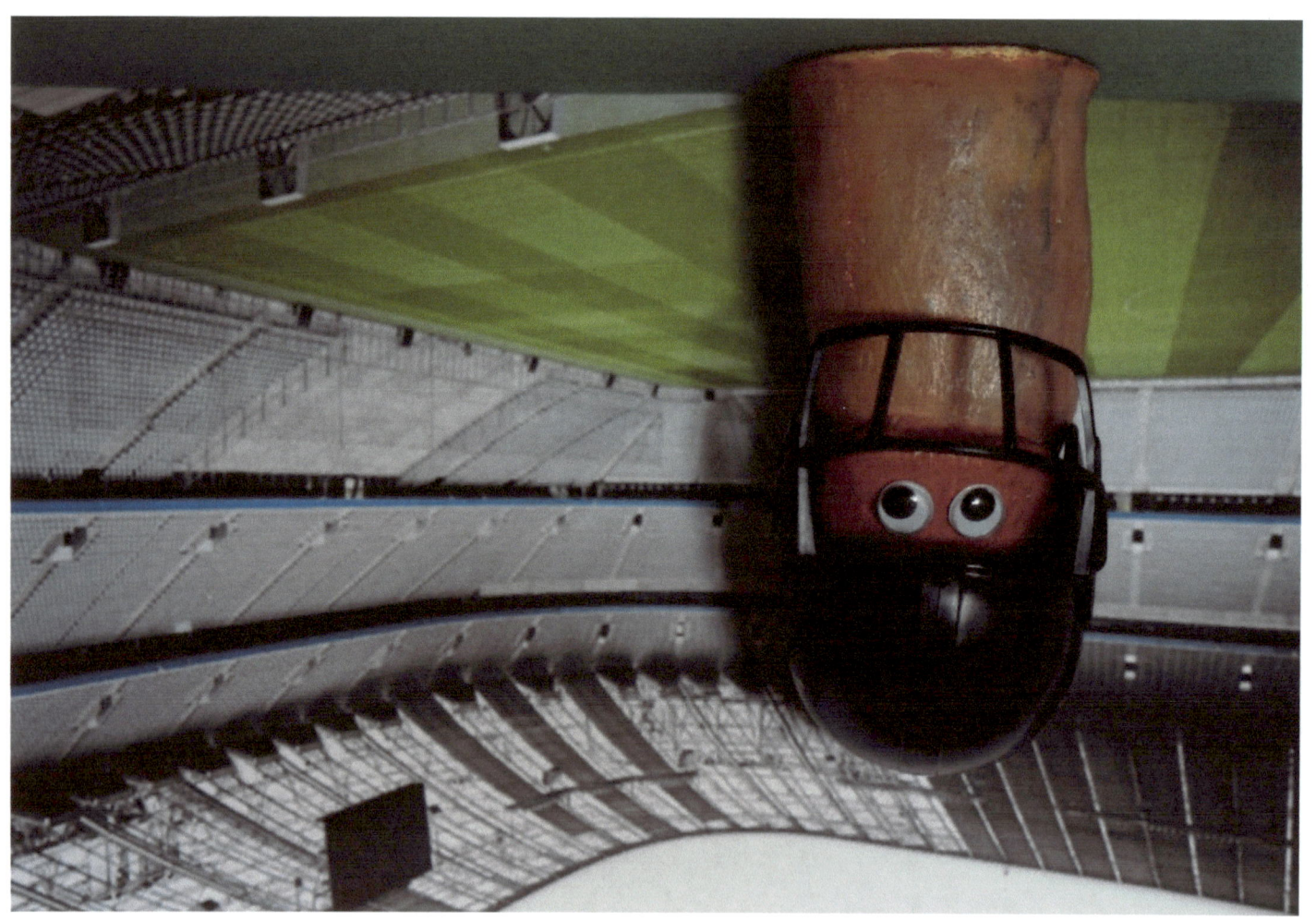

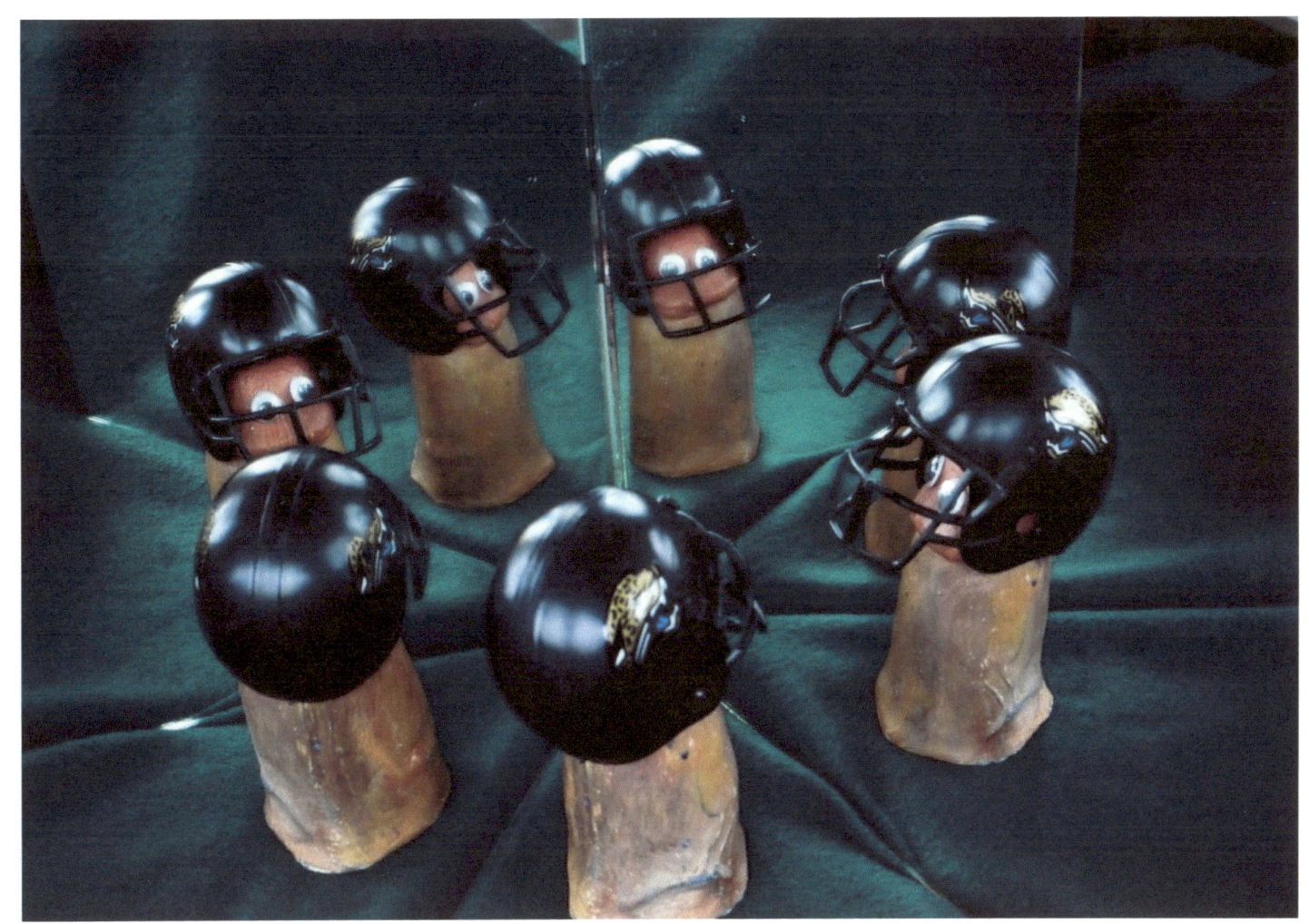

THE HUDDLE

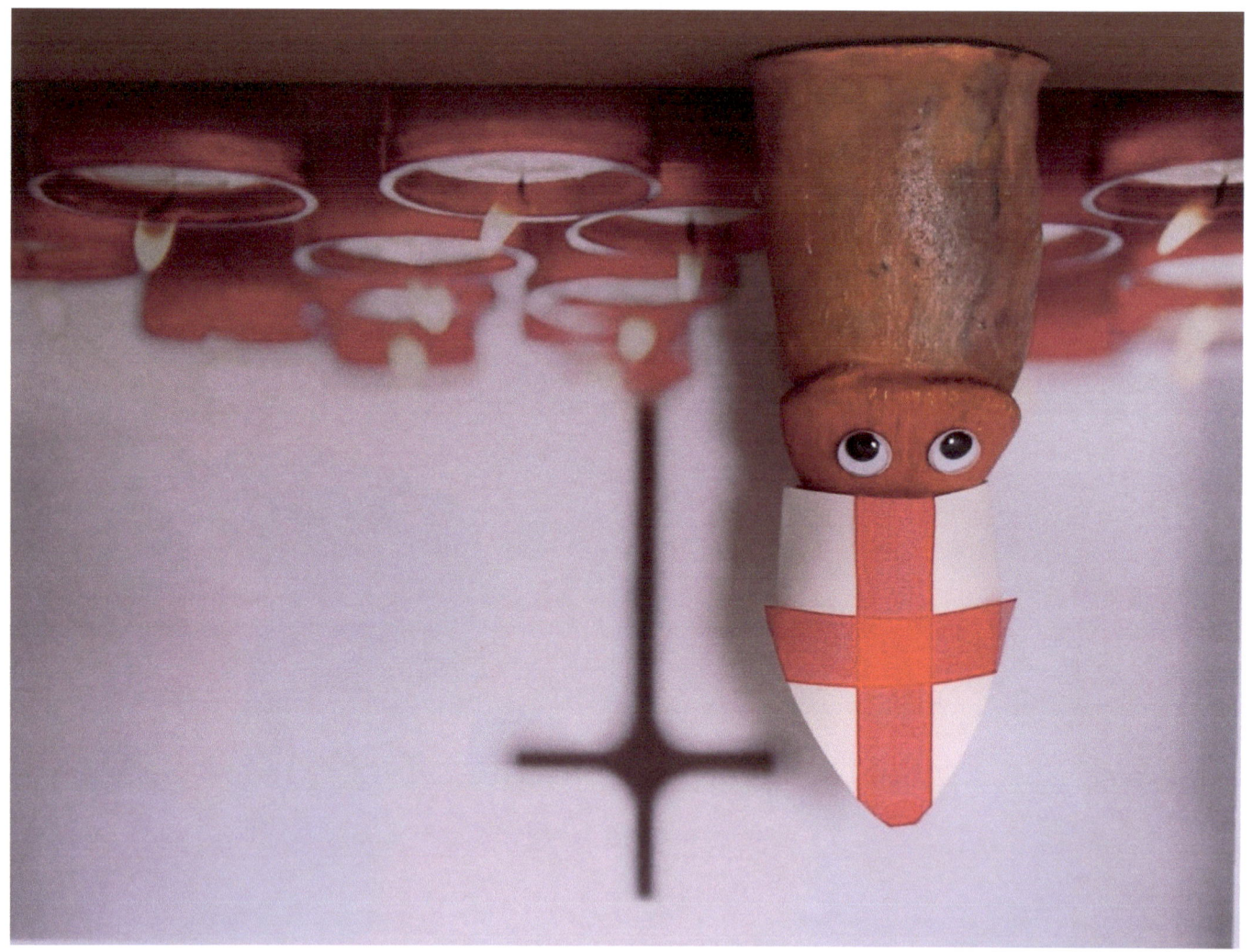

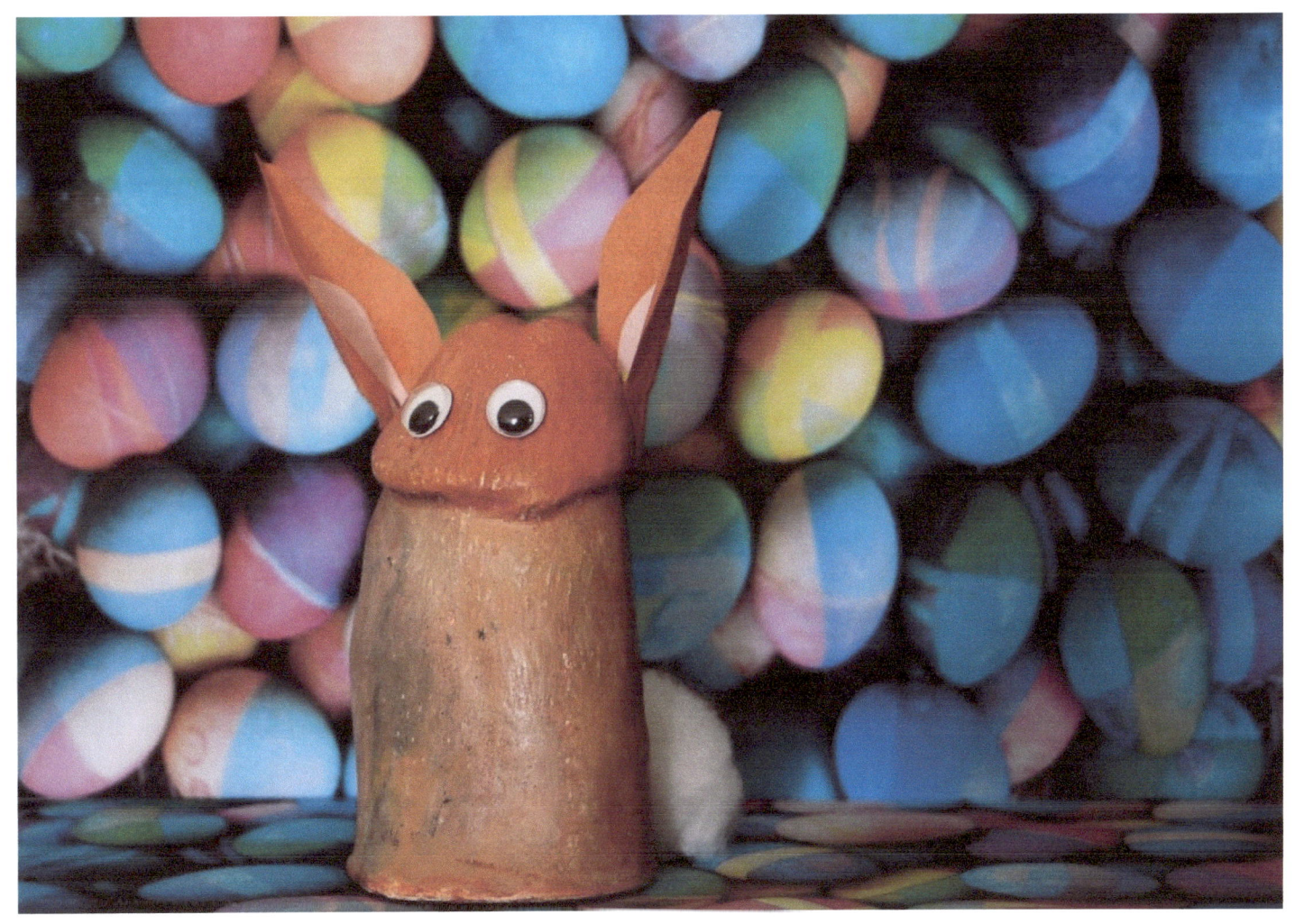

PETER COTTONTAIL

COCKATOO

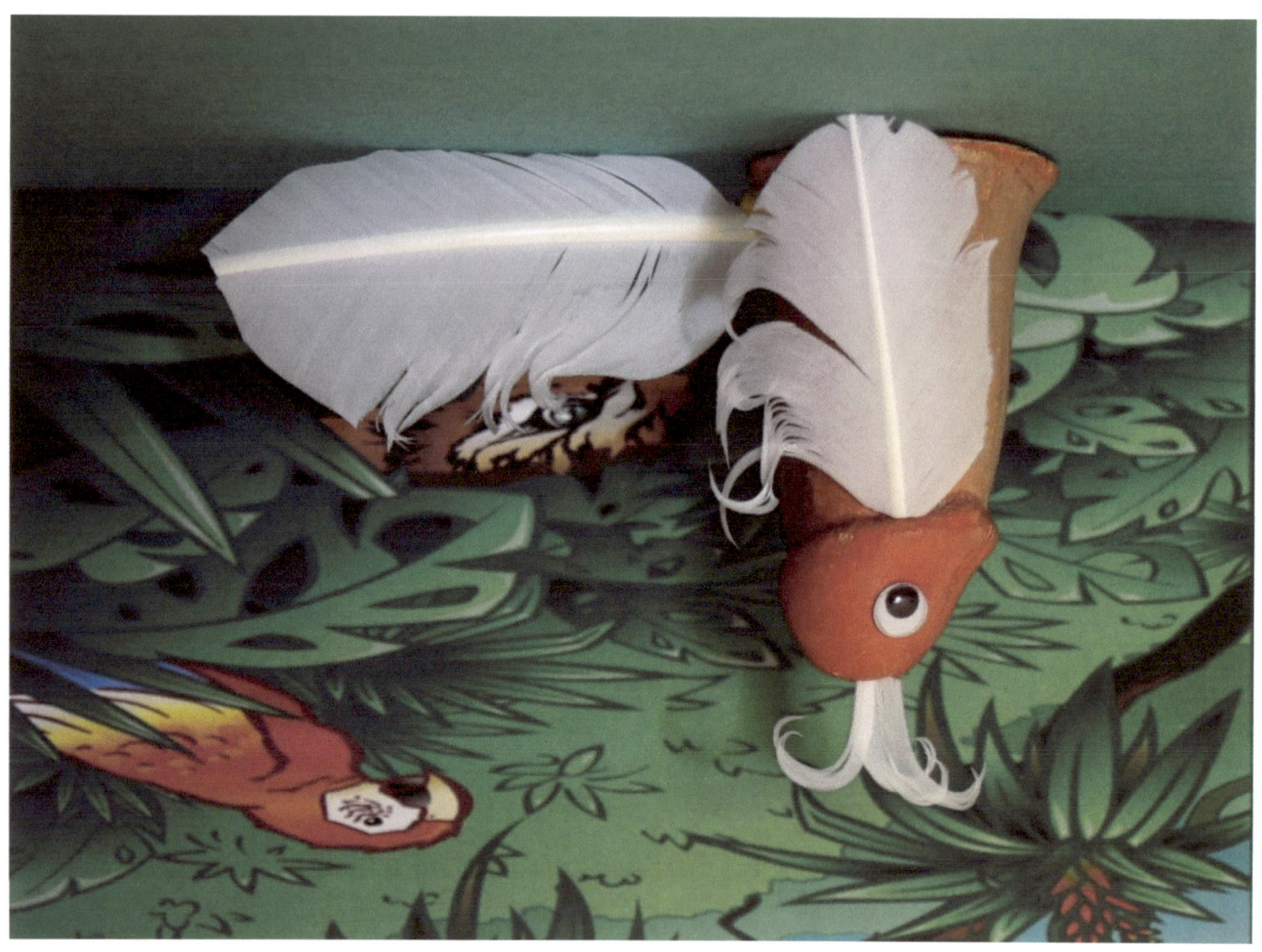

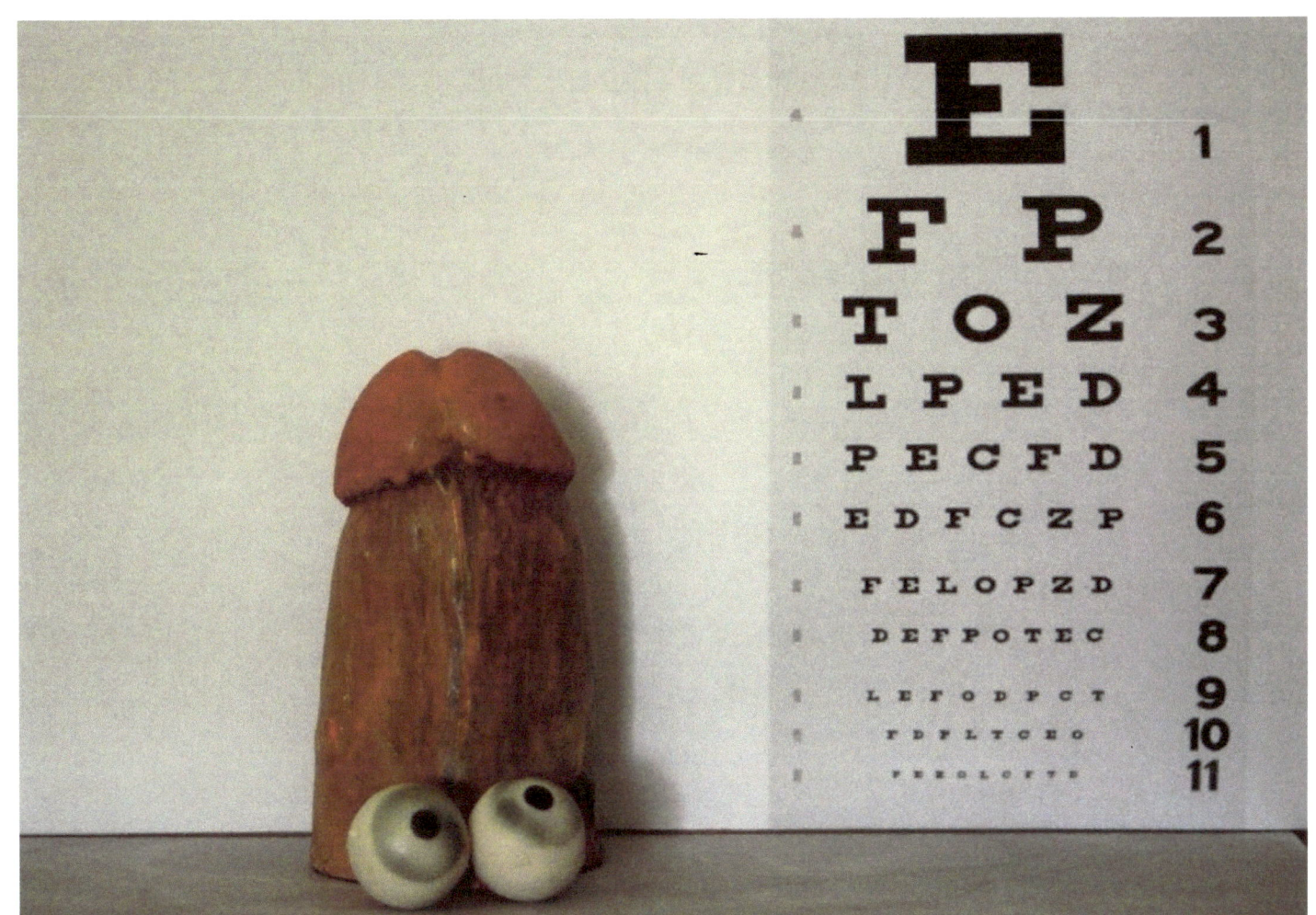

EYEBALLS

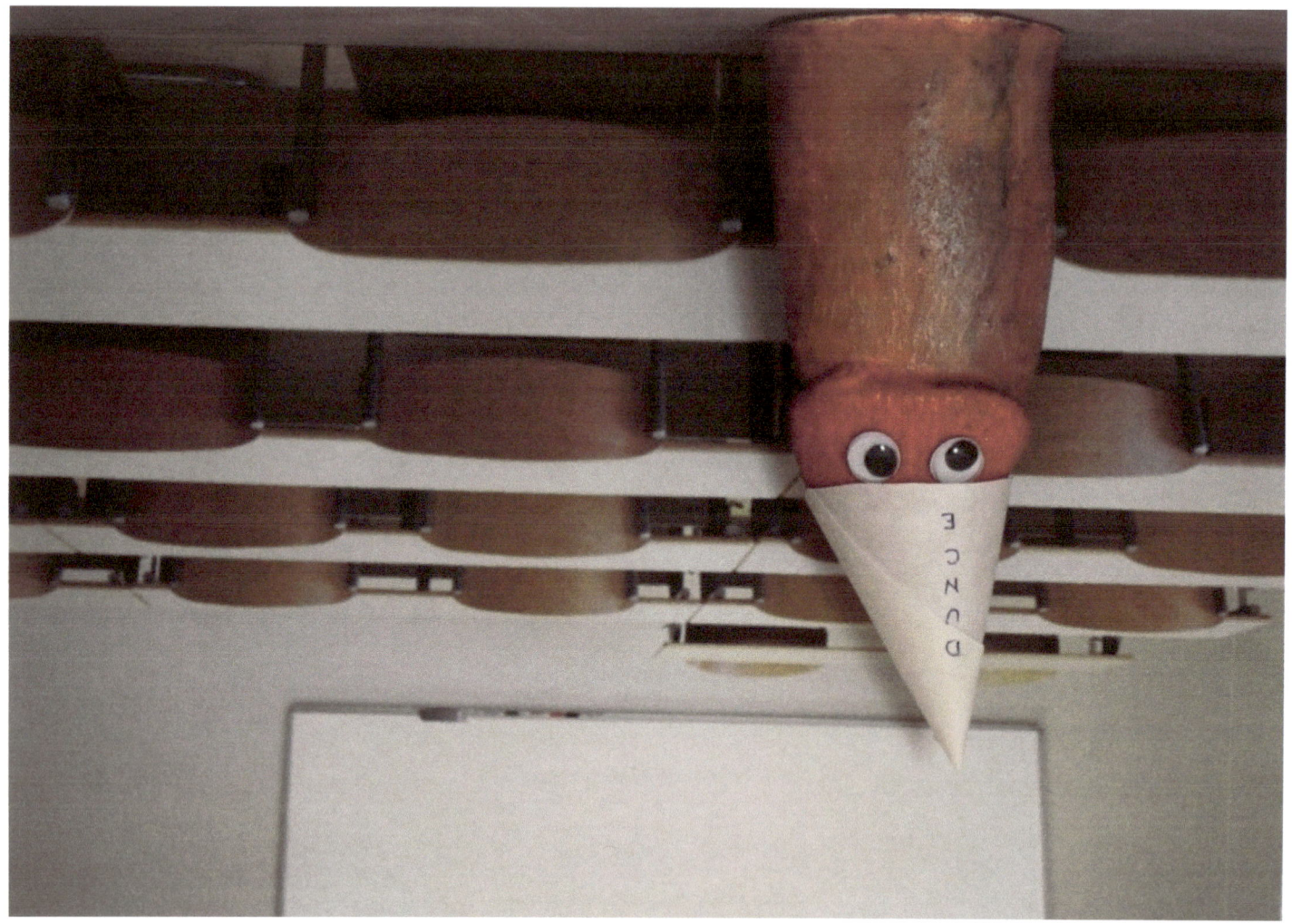

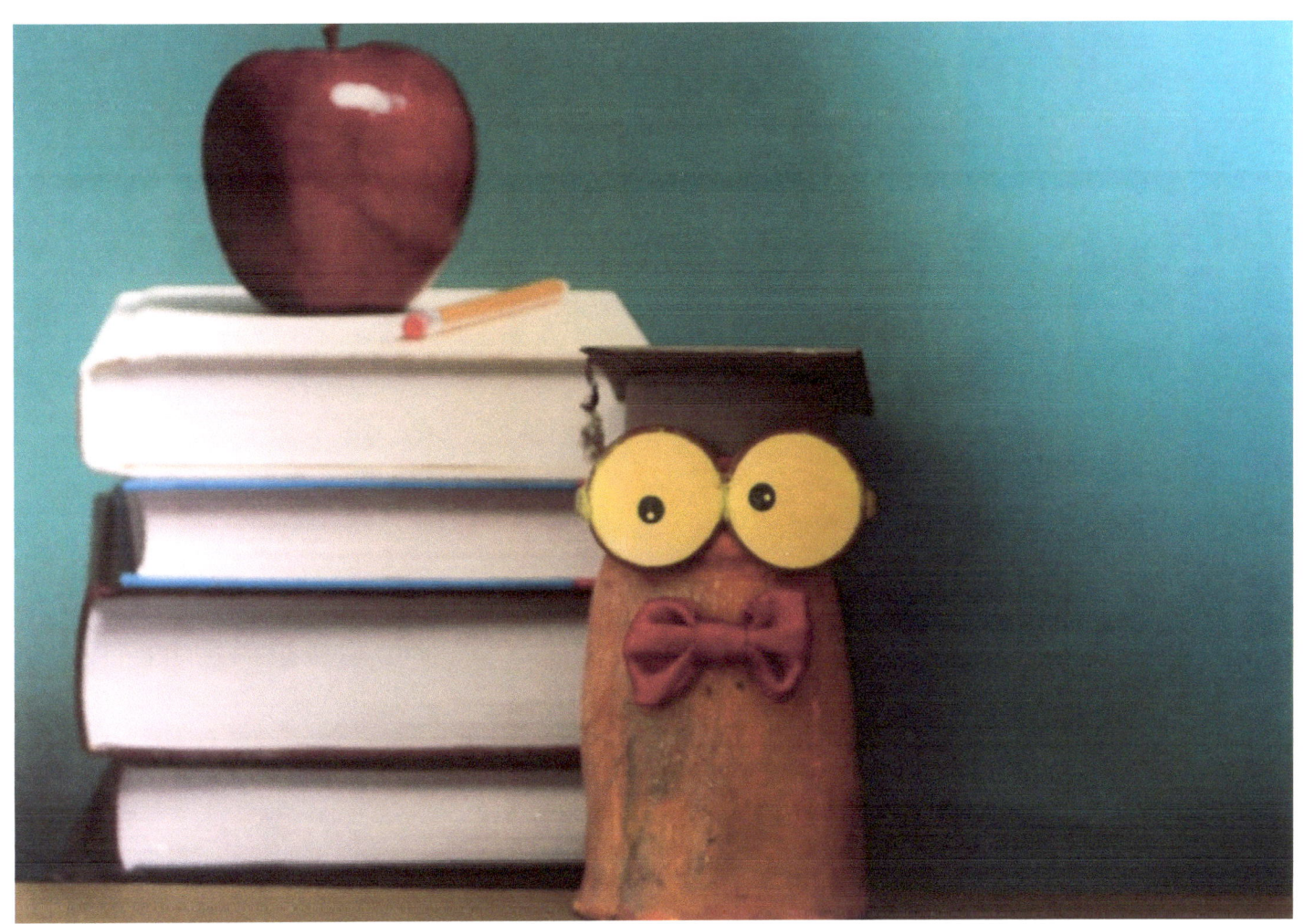

SMART ONE

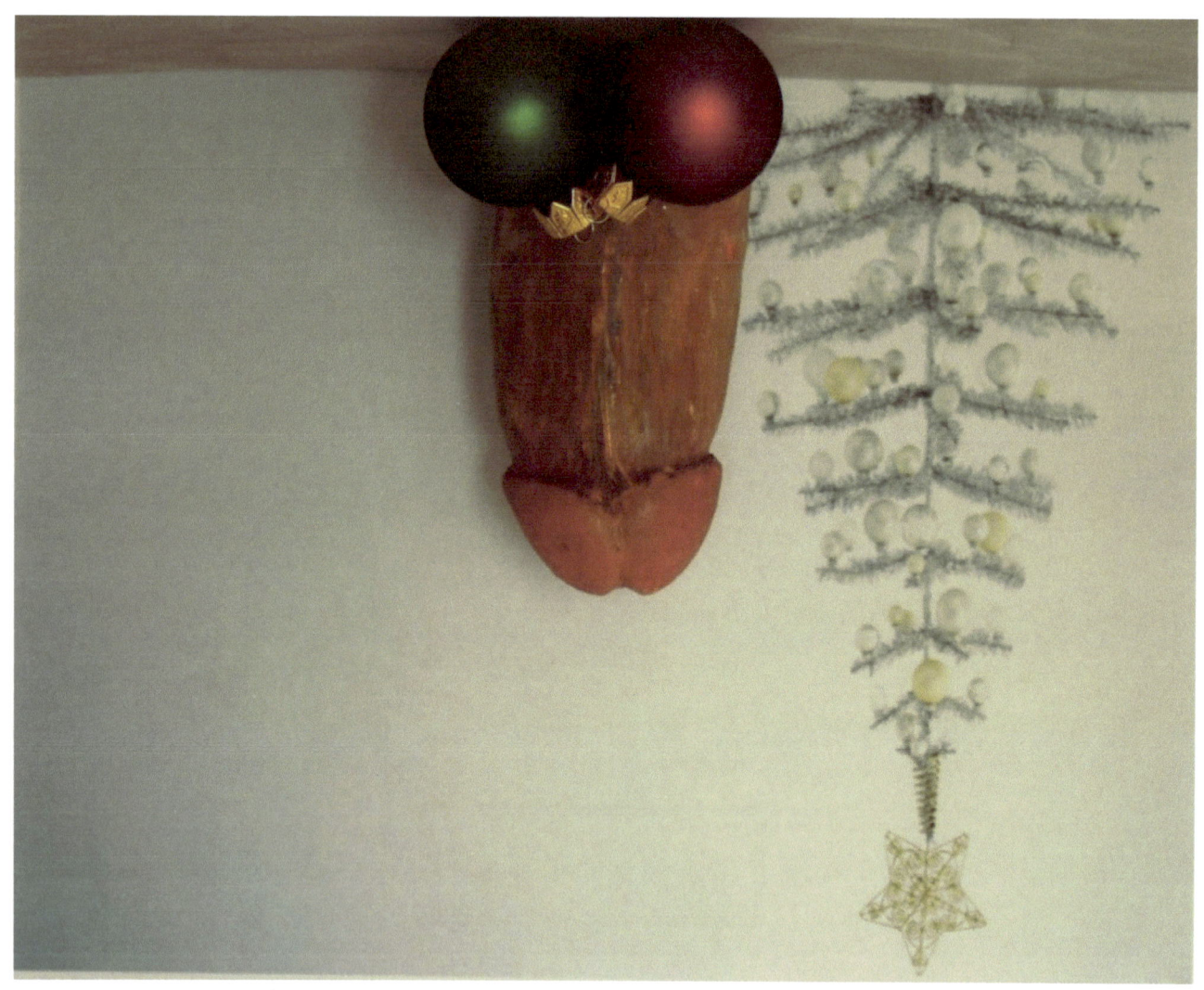

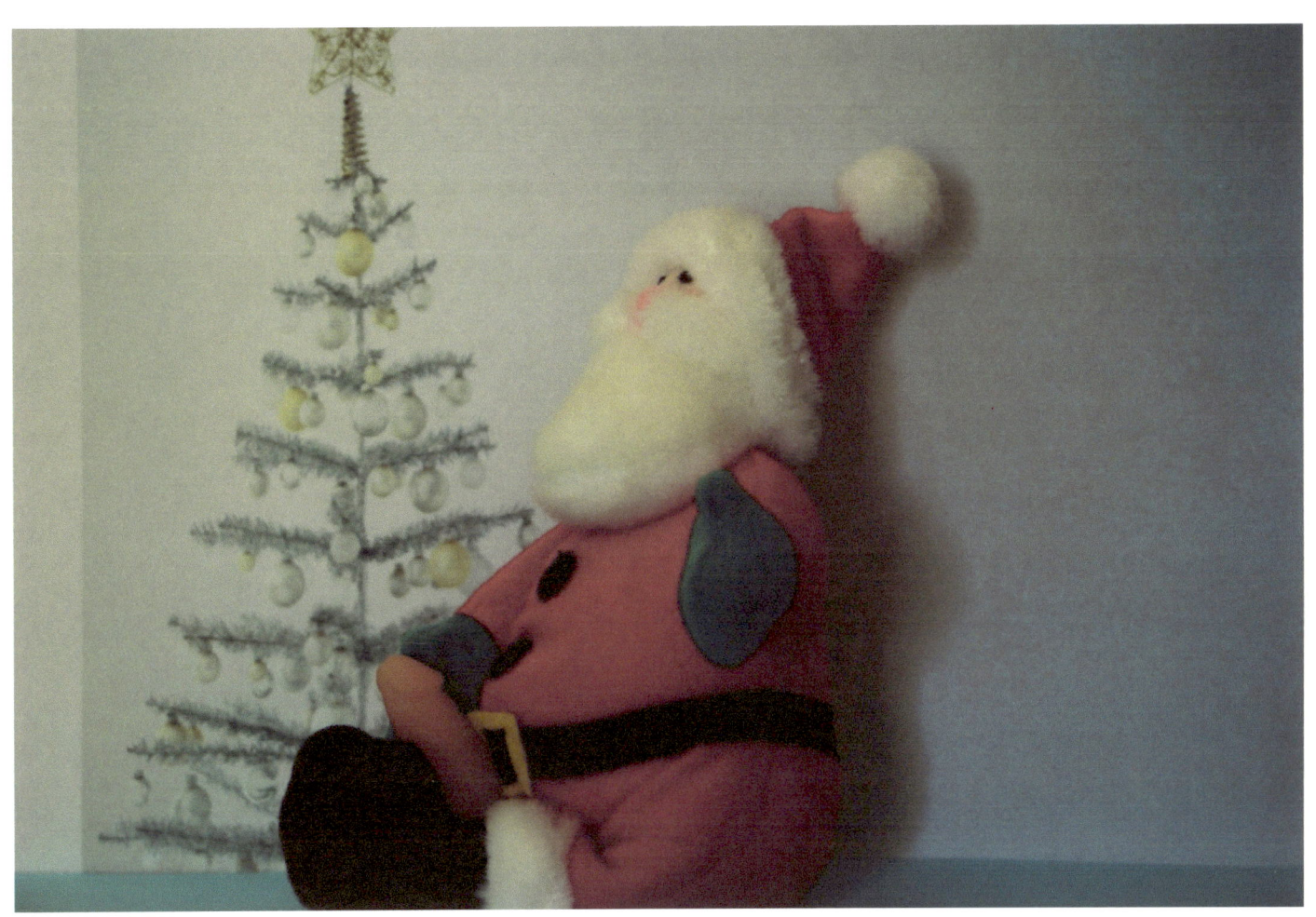

SANTA CLAUS IS COMING

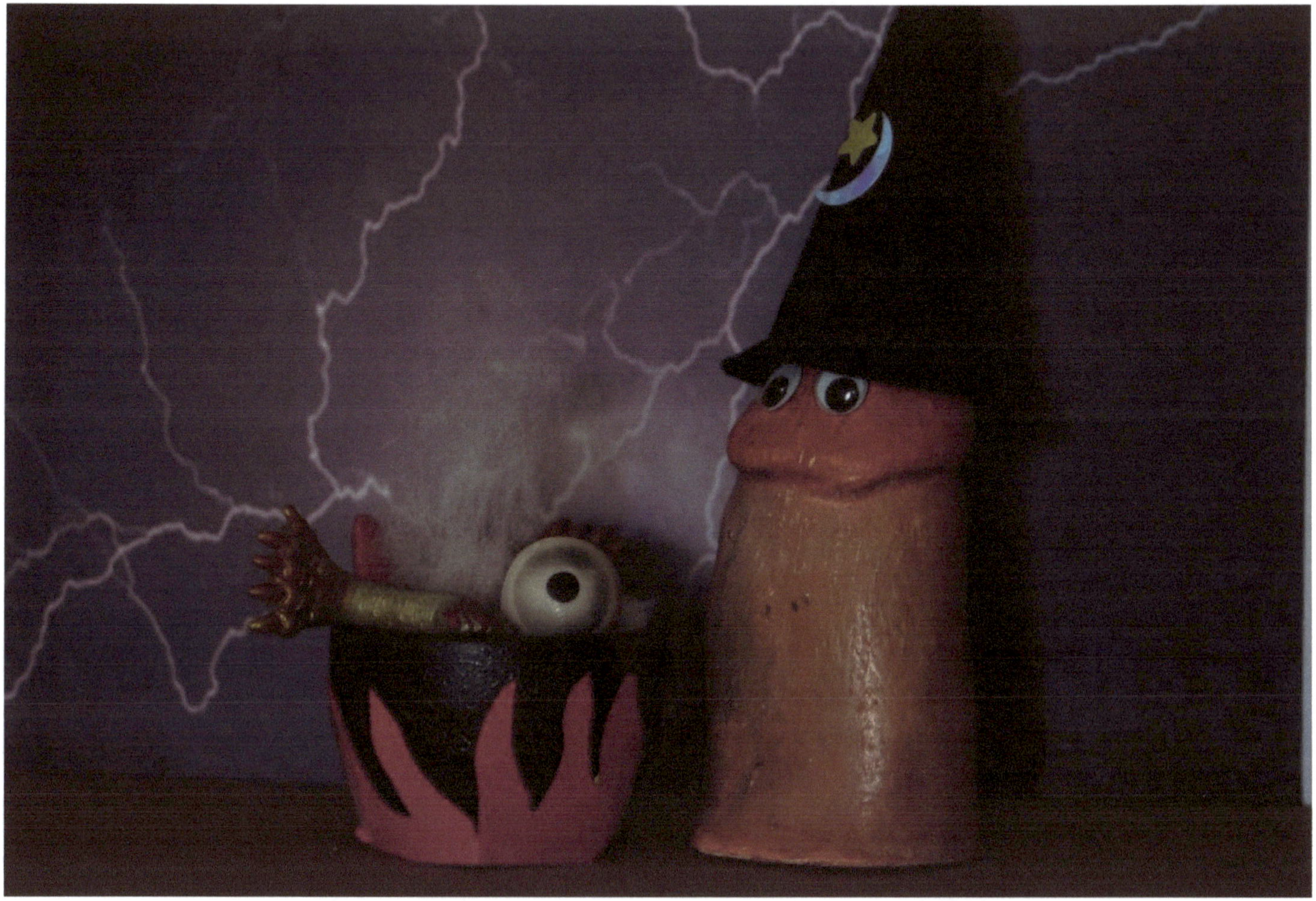

Wizard of Id—Alchemist

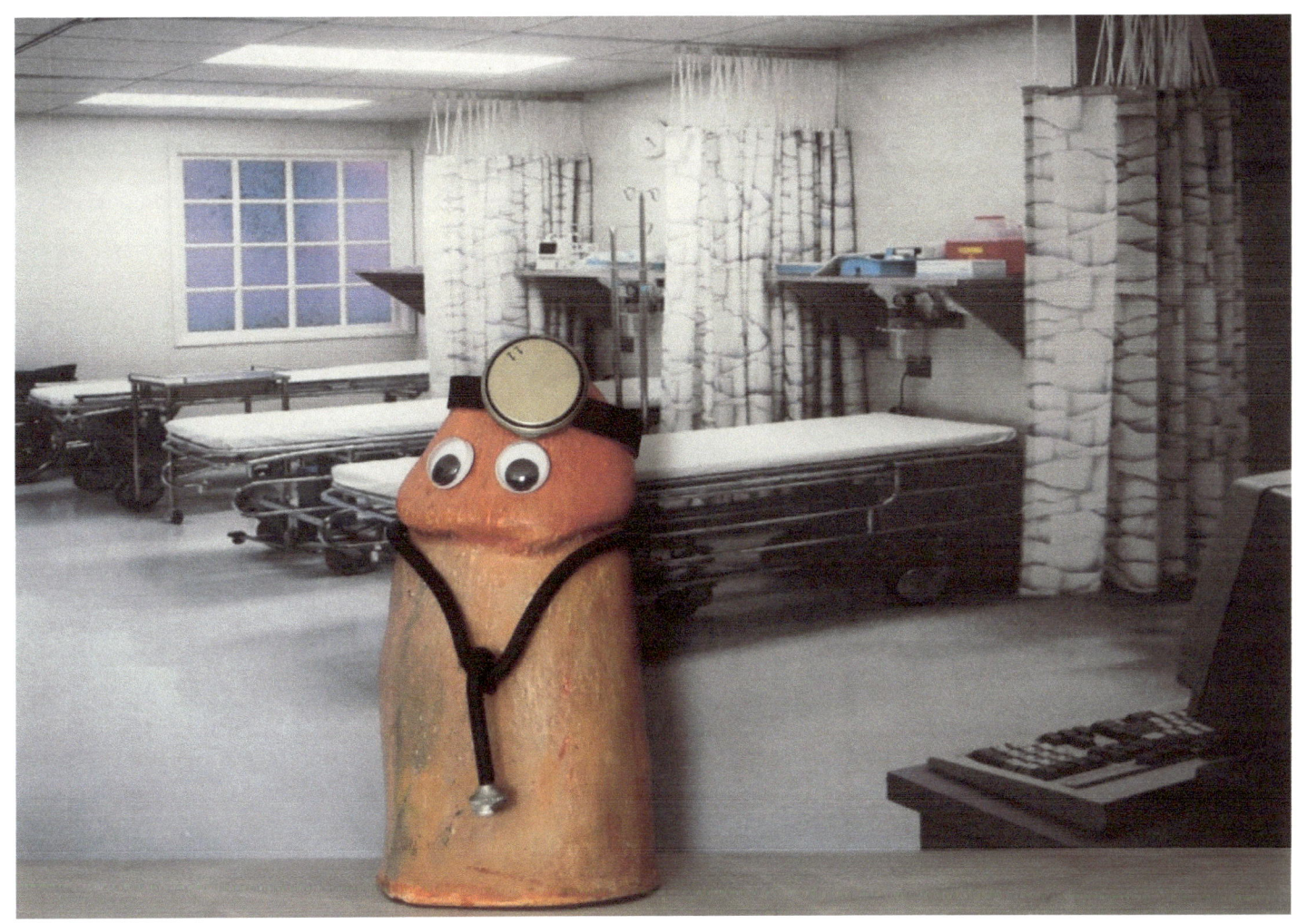

PROCTOLOGIST

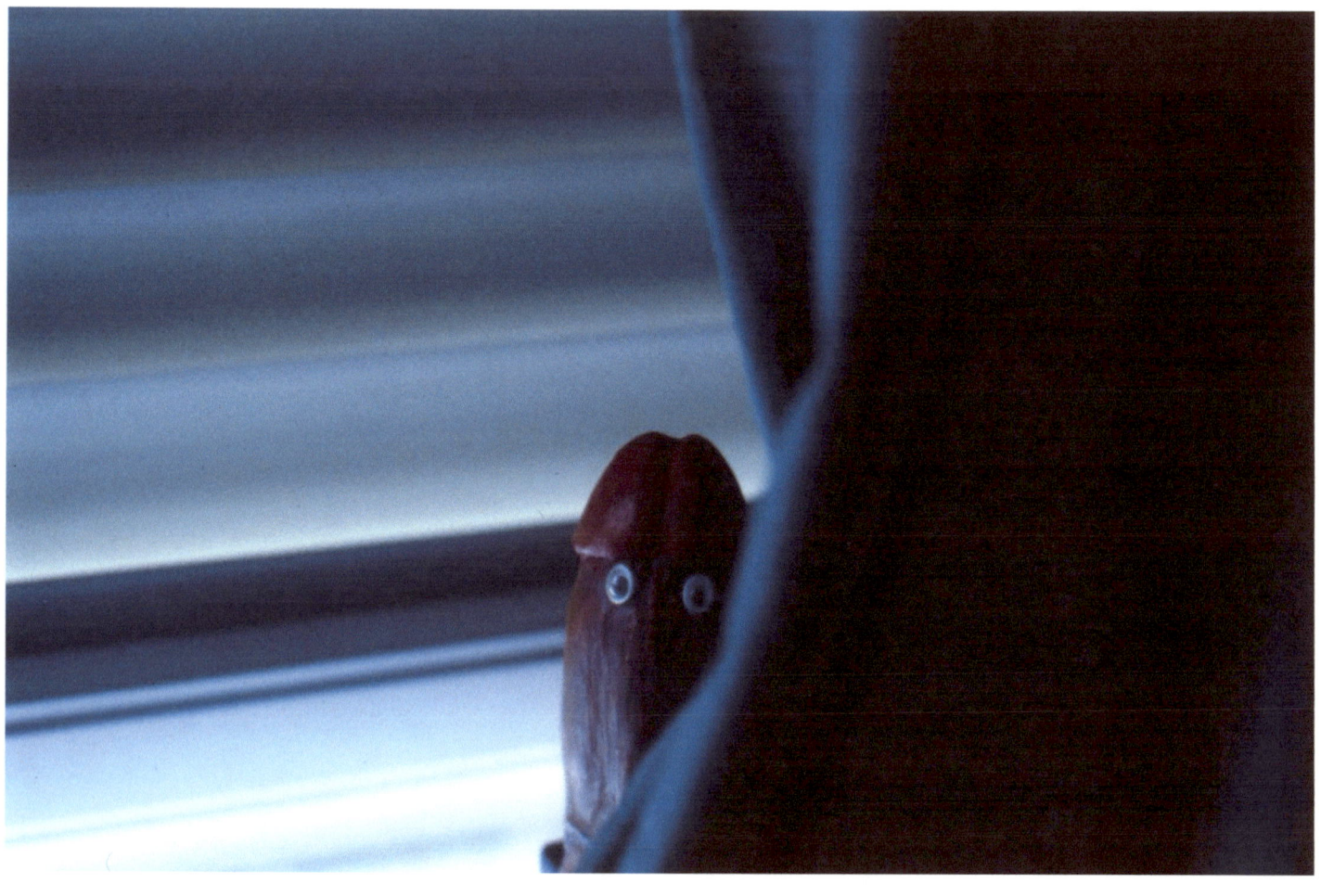

PEEKING DICK

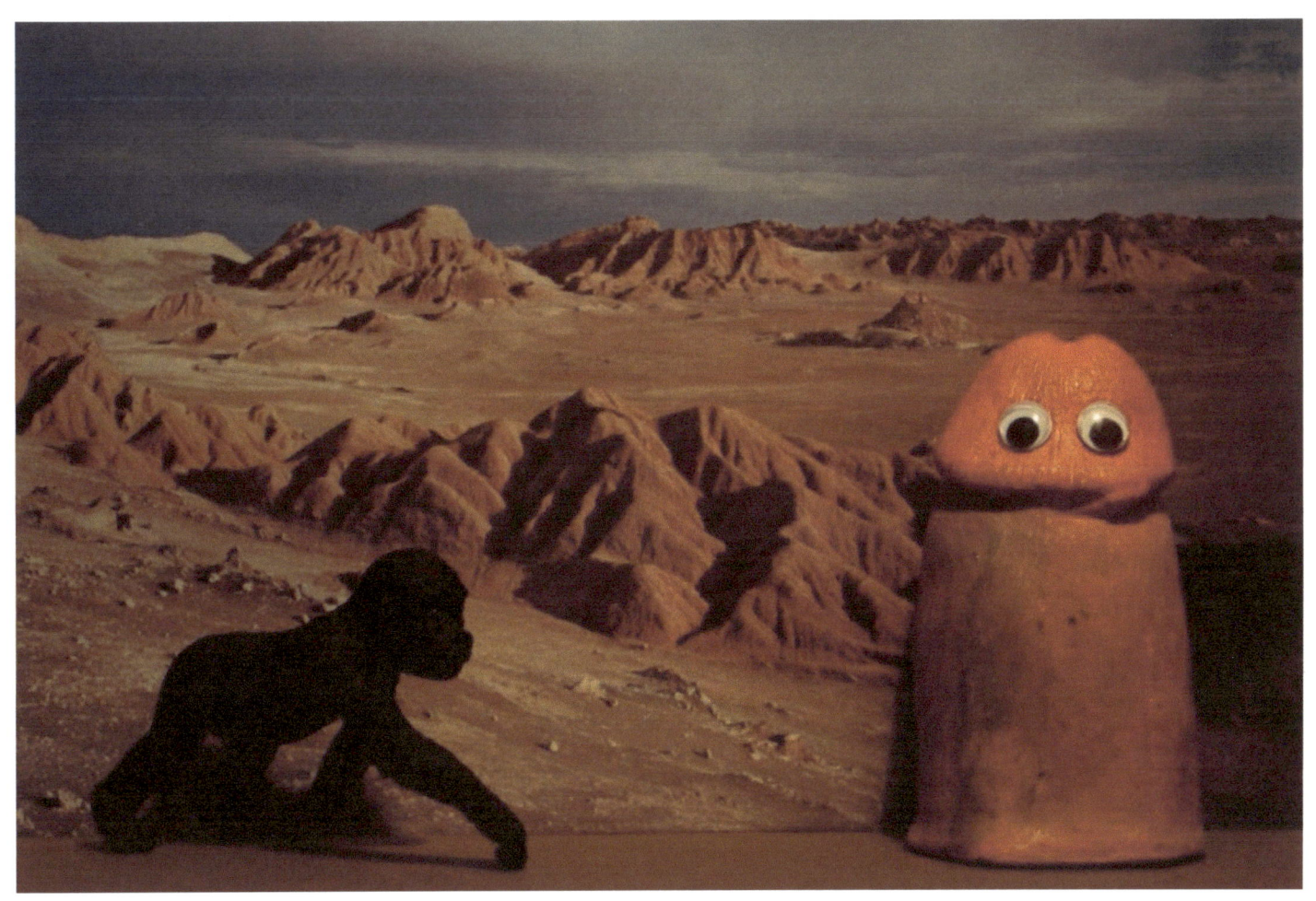

2 MILLION YEARS OF EVOLUTION

HOMO HABILIS TO HOMO ERECTUS

JAIL BIRD

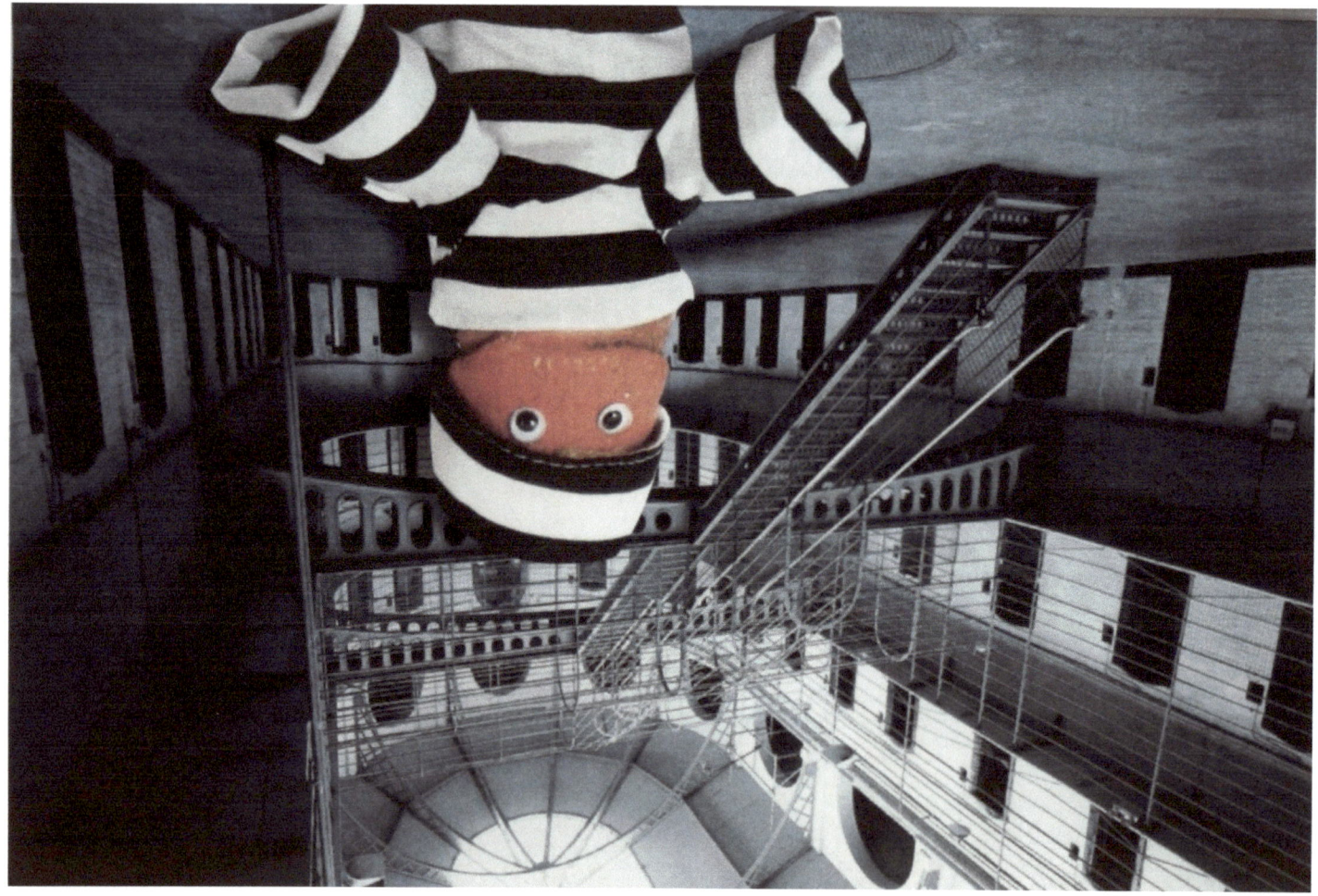

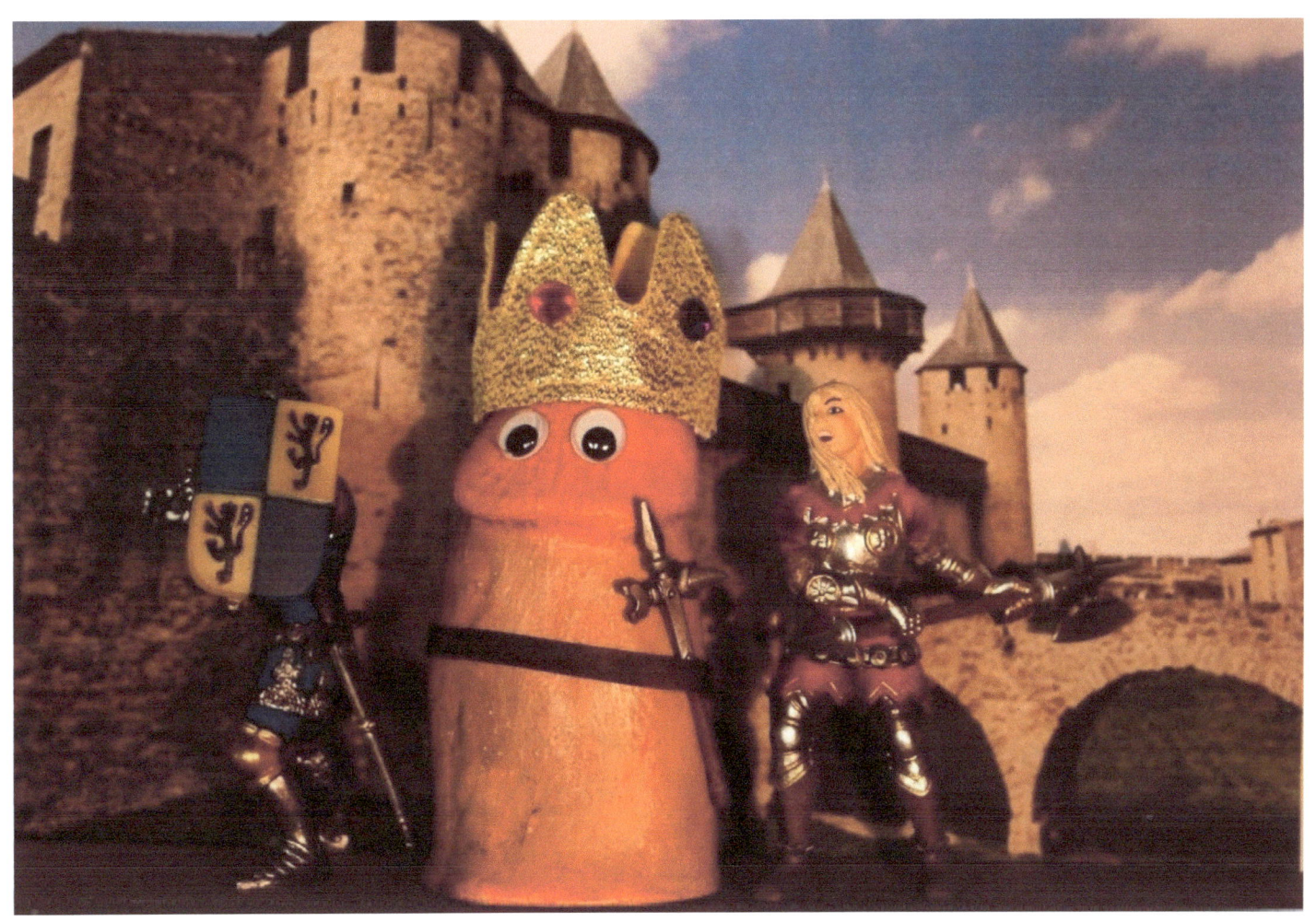

DICKEY THE LIONHEARTED

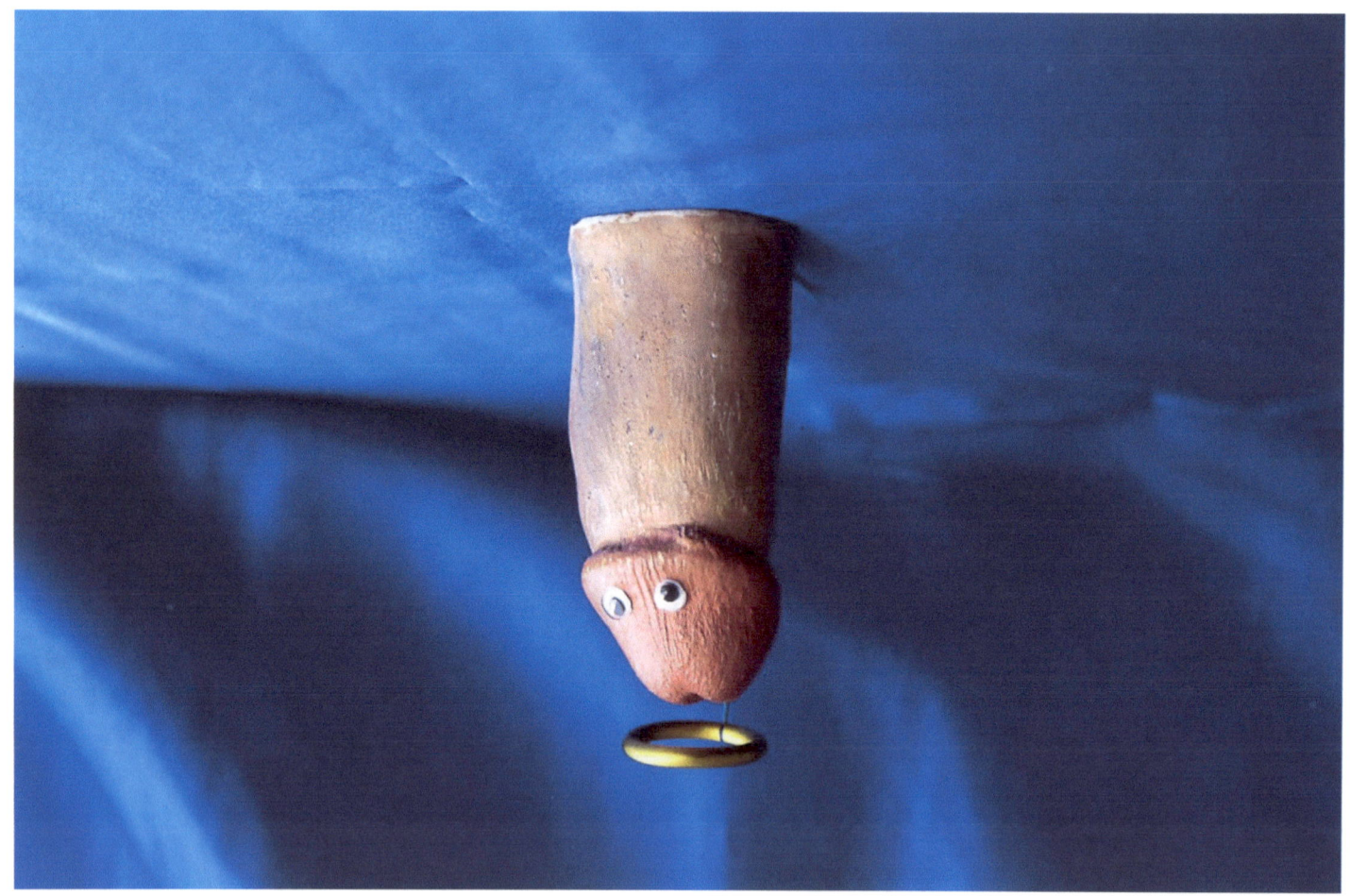

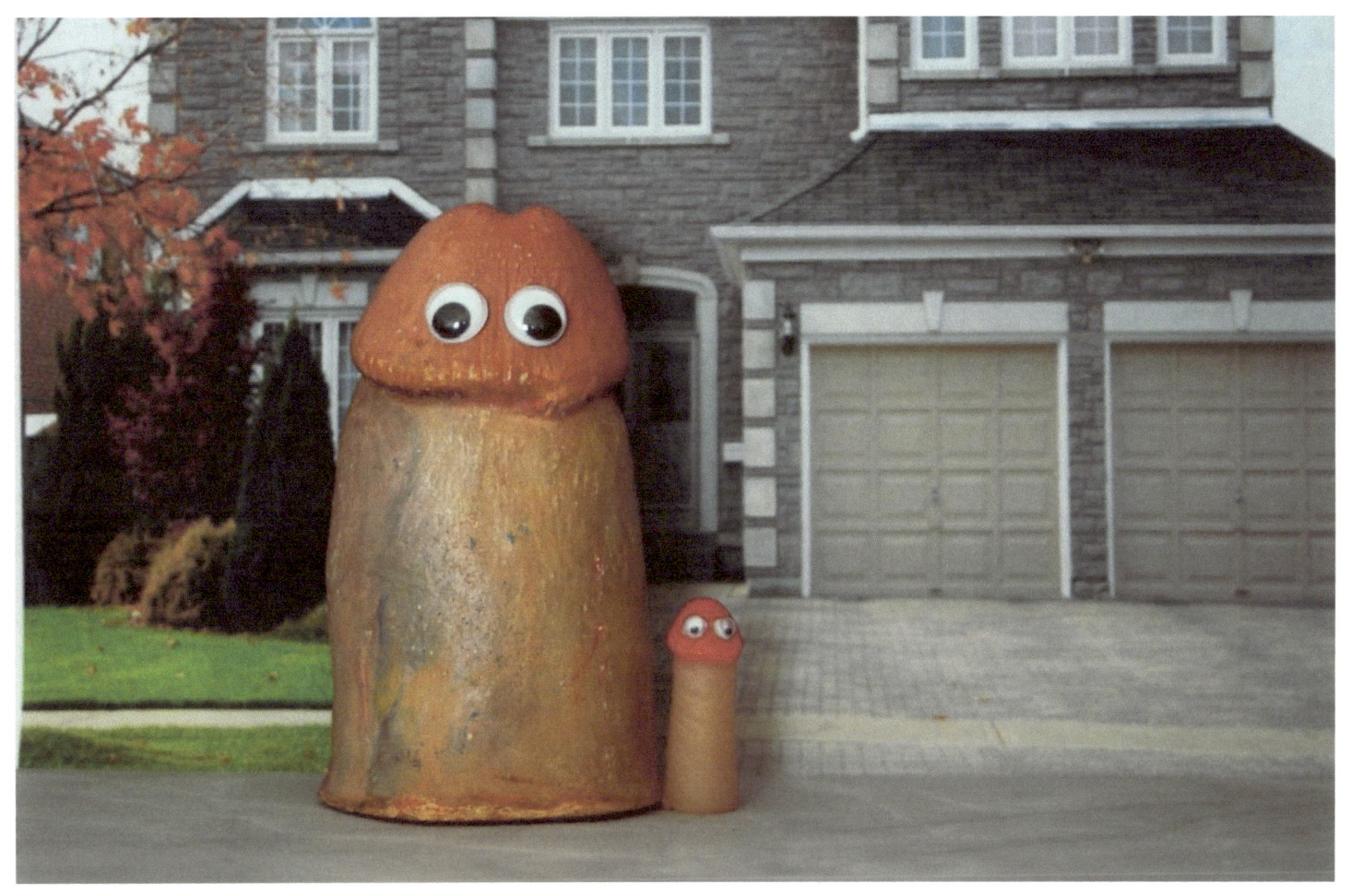

CHIP OFF THE OLD COCK

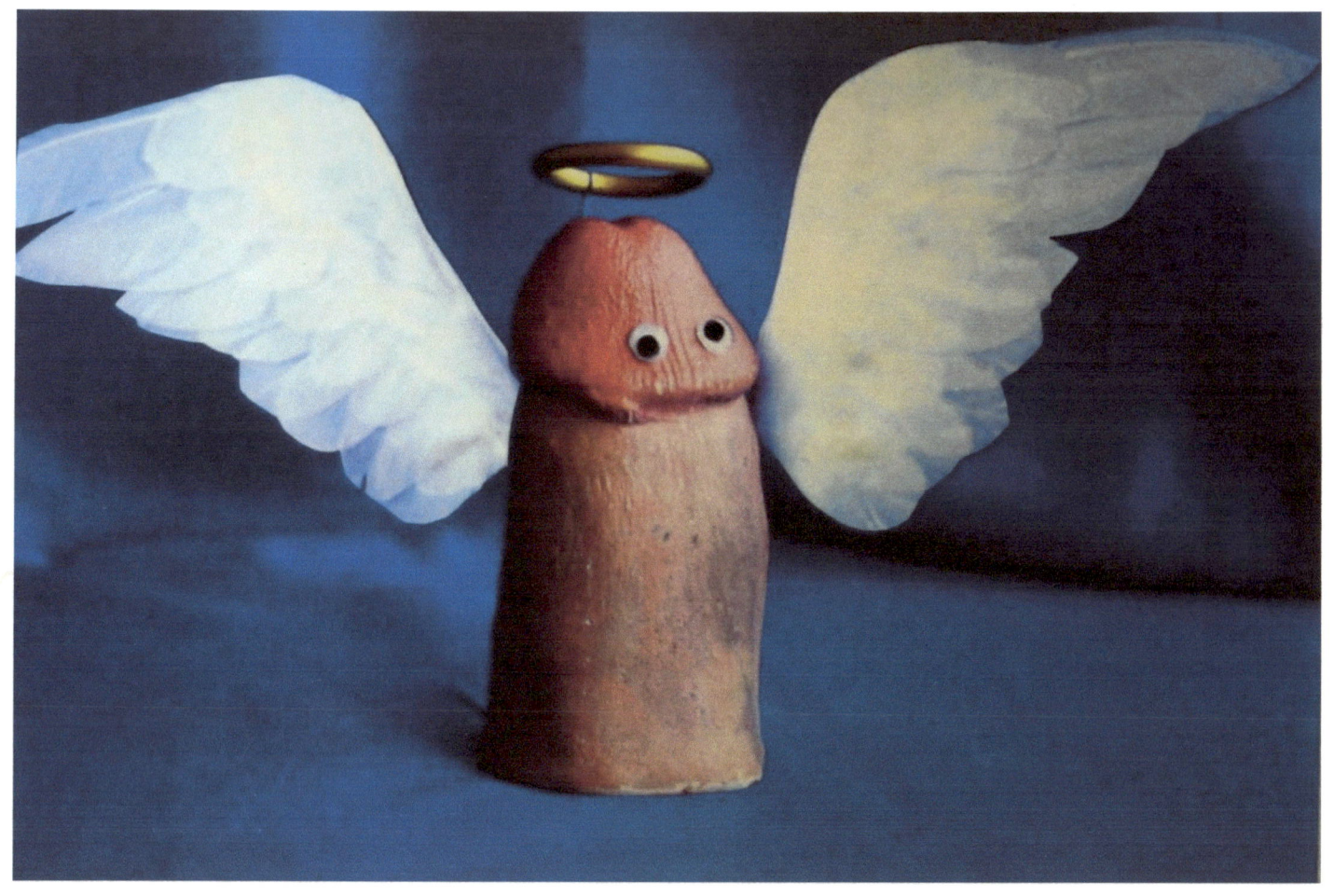

GUARDIAN ANGEL FOR GAYS

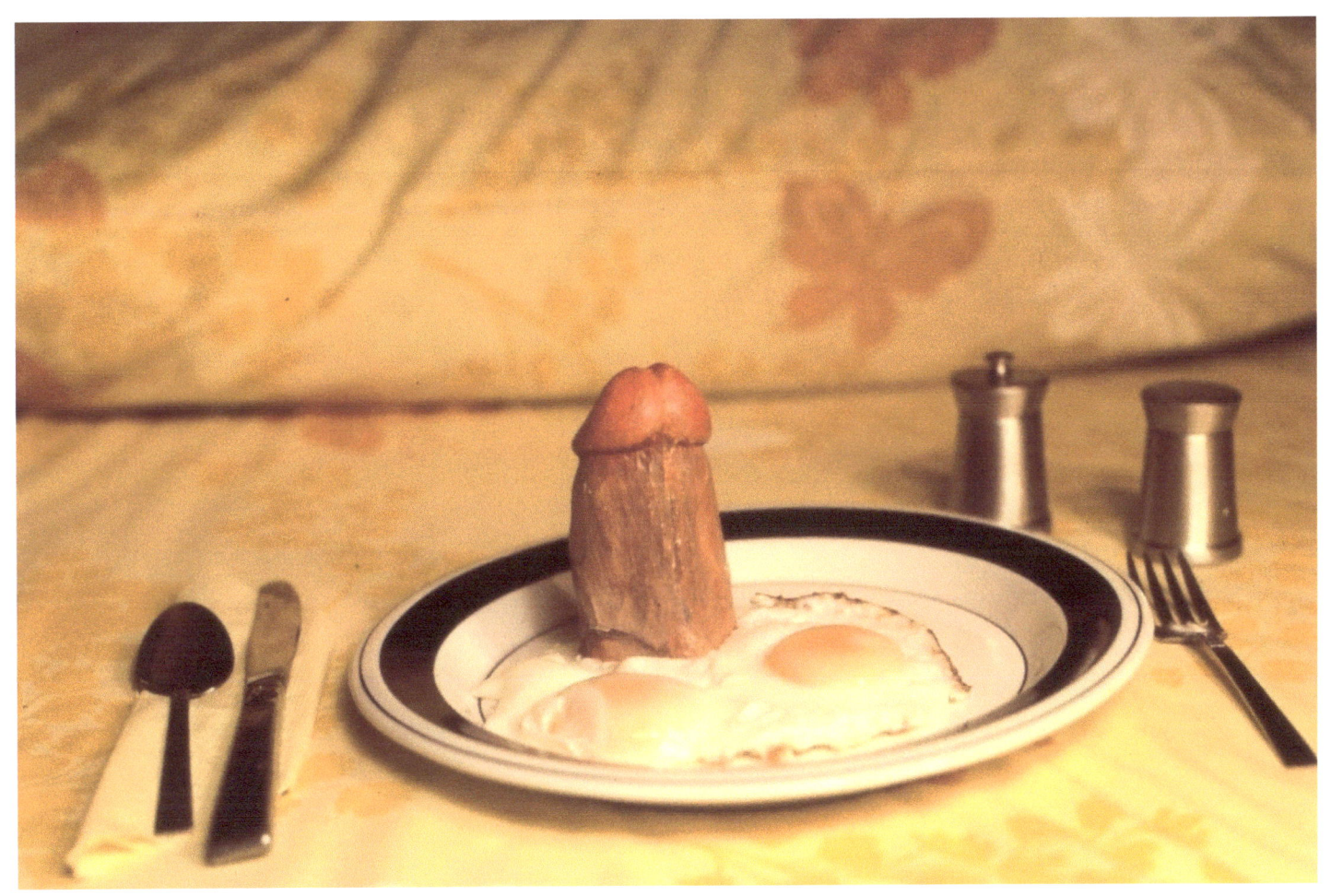

BREAKFAST AT STIFFANIES

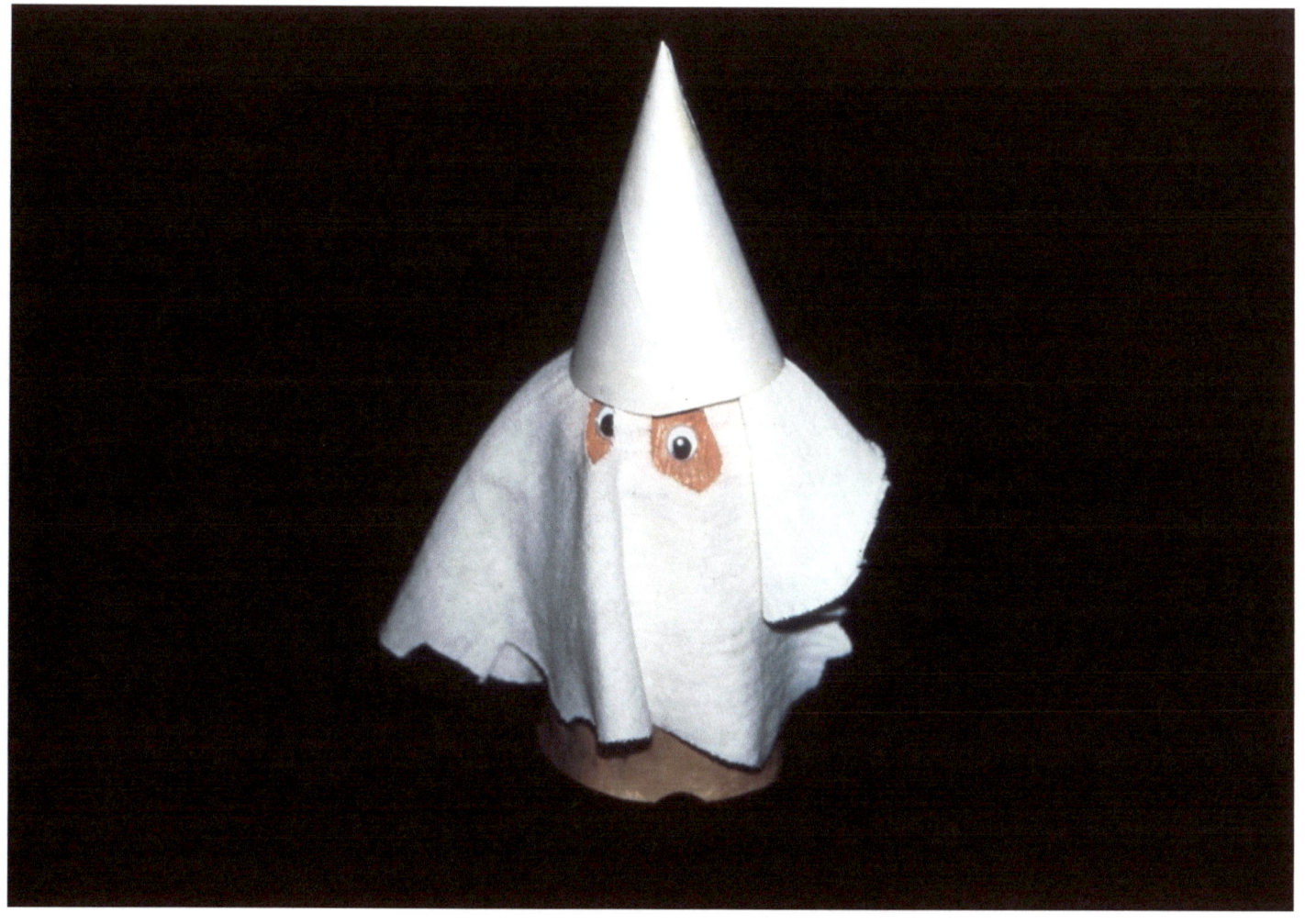

KOOK COCK CLAN

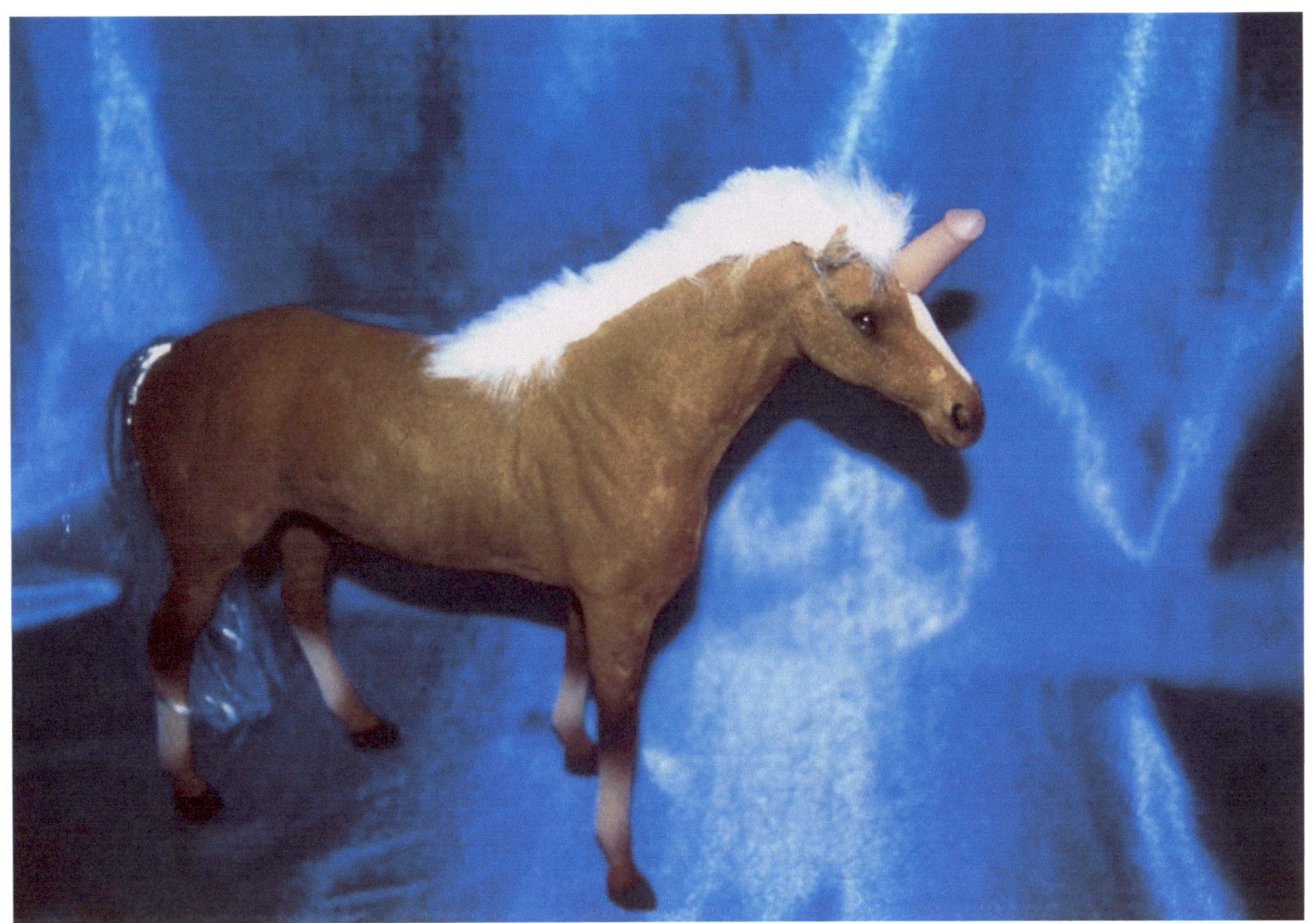

UNICOCK

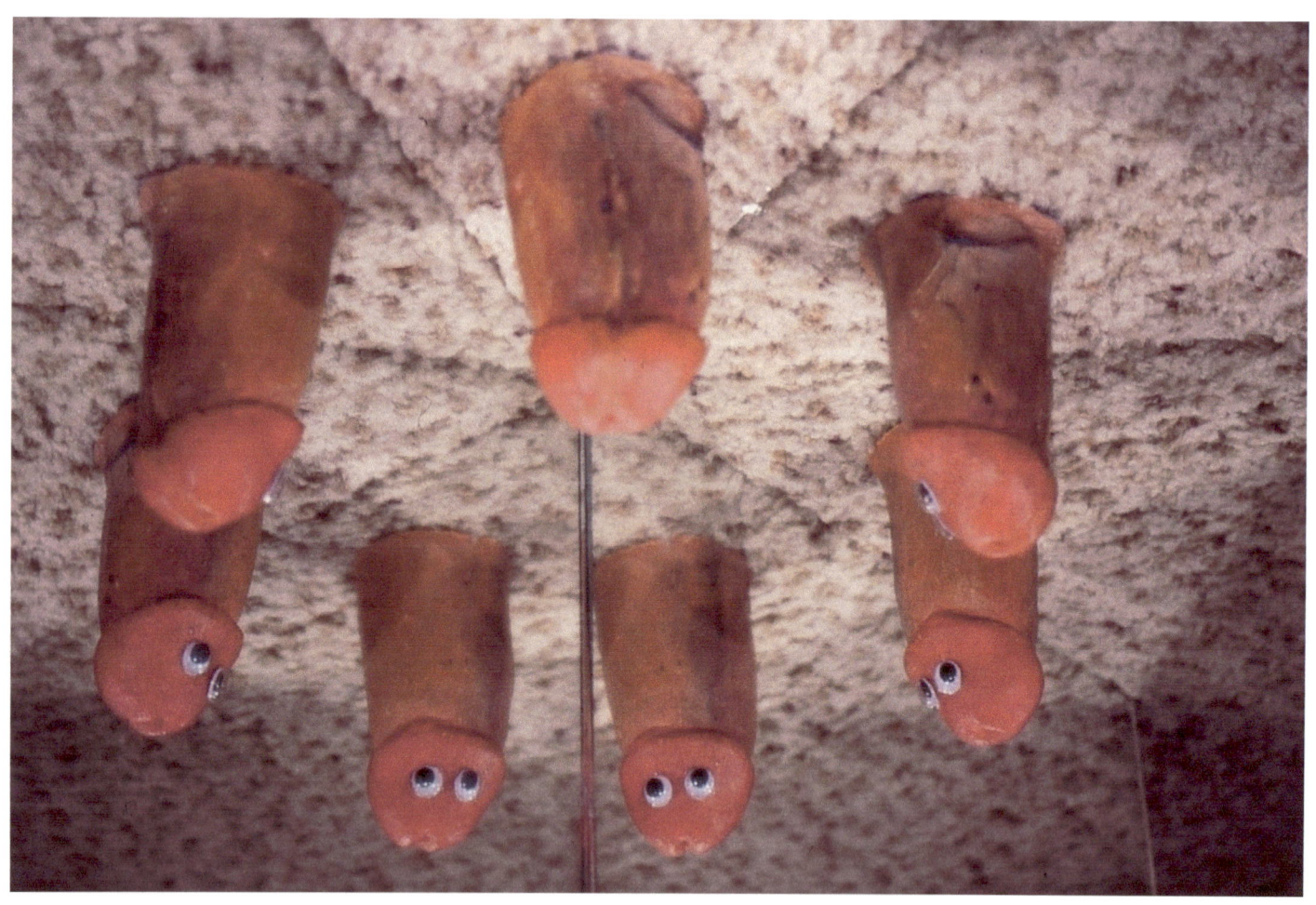

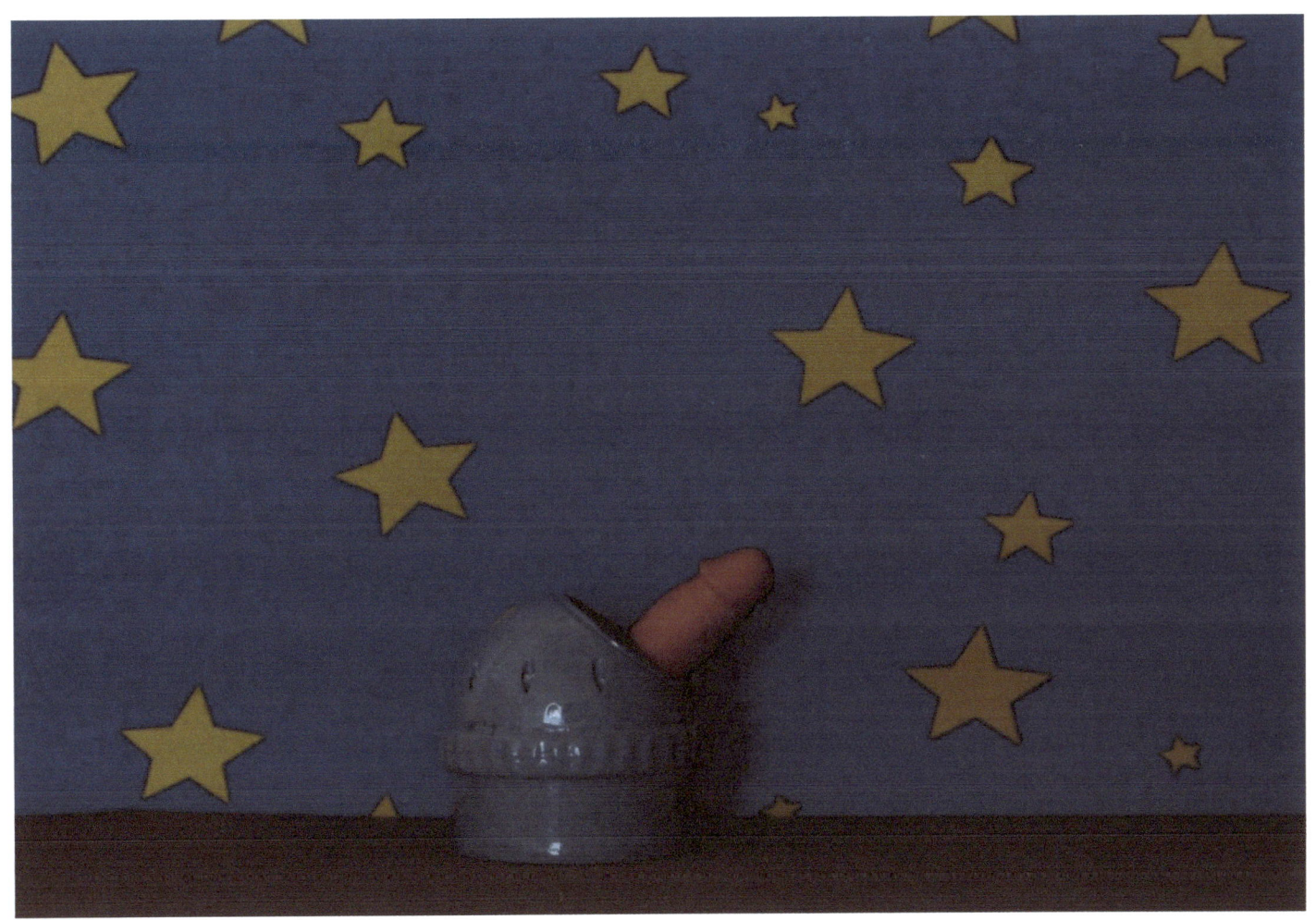

MOUNT PENIS

LEANING TOWER OF PENIS

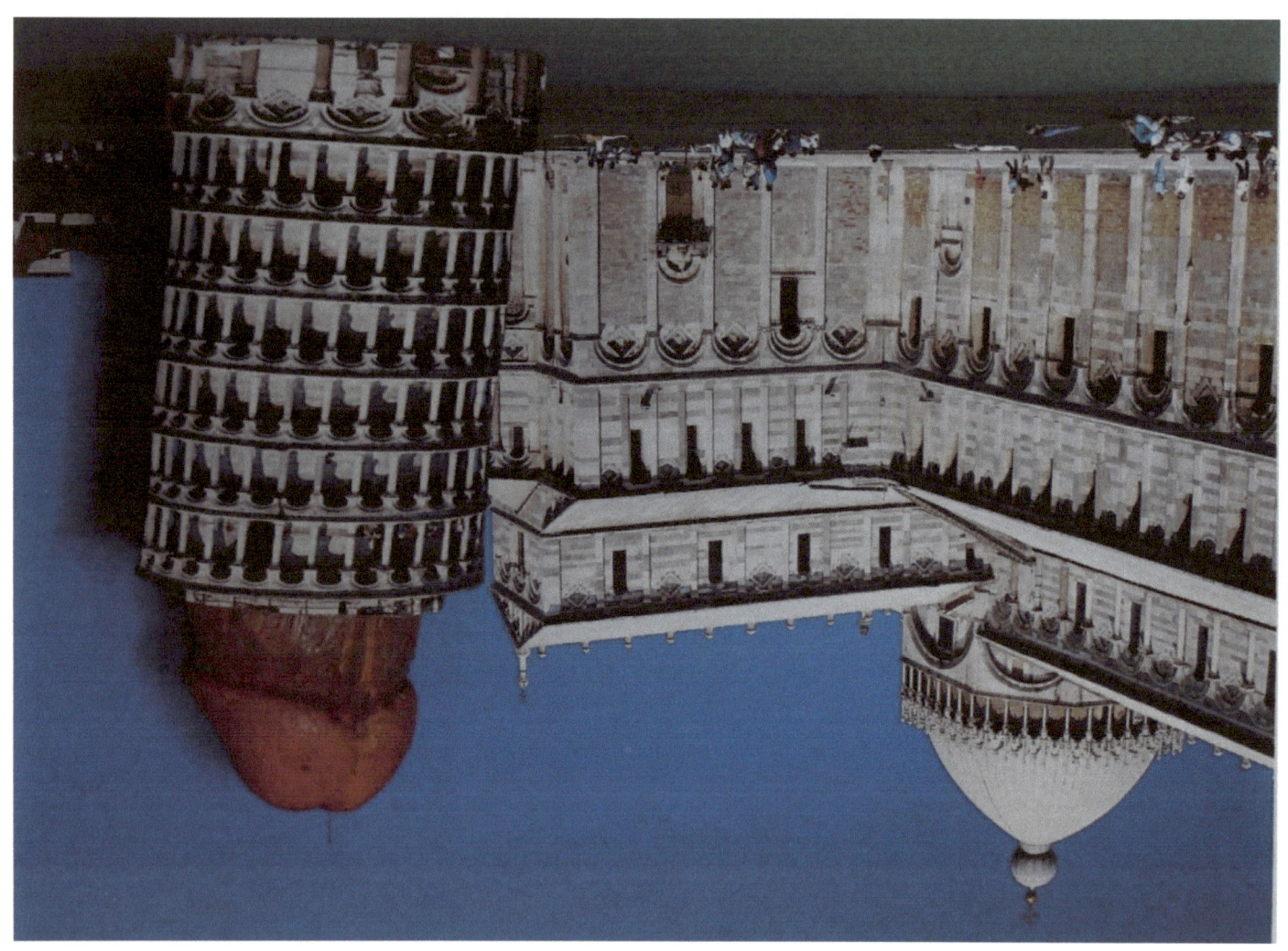

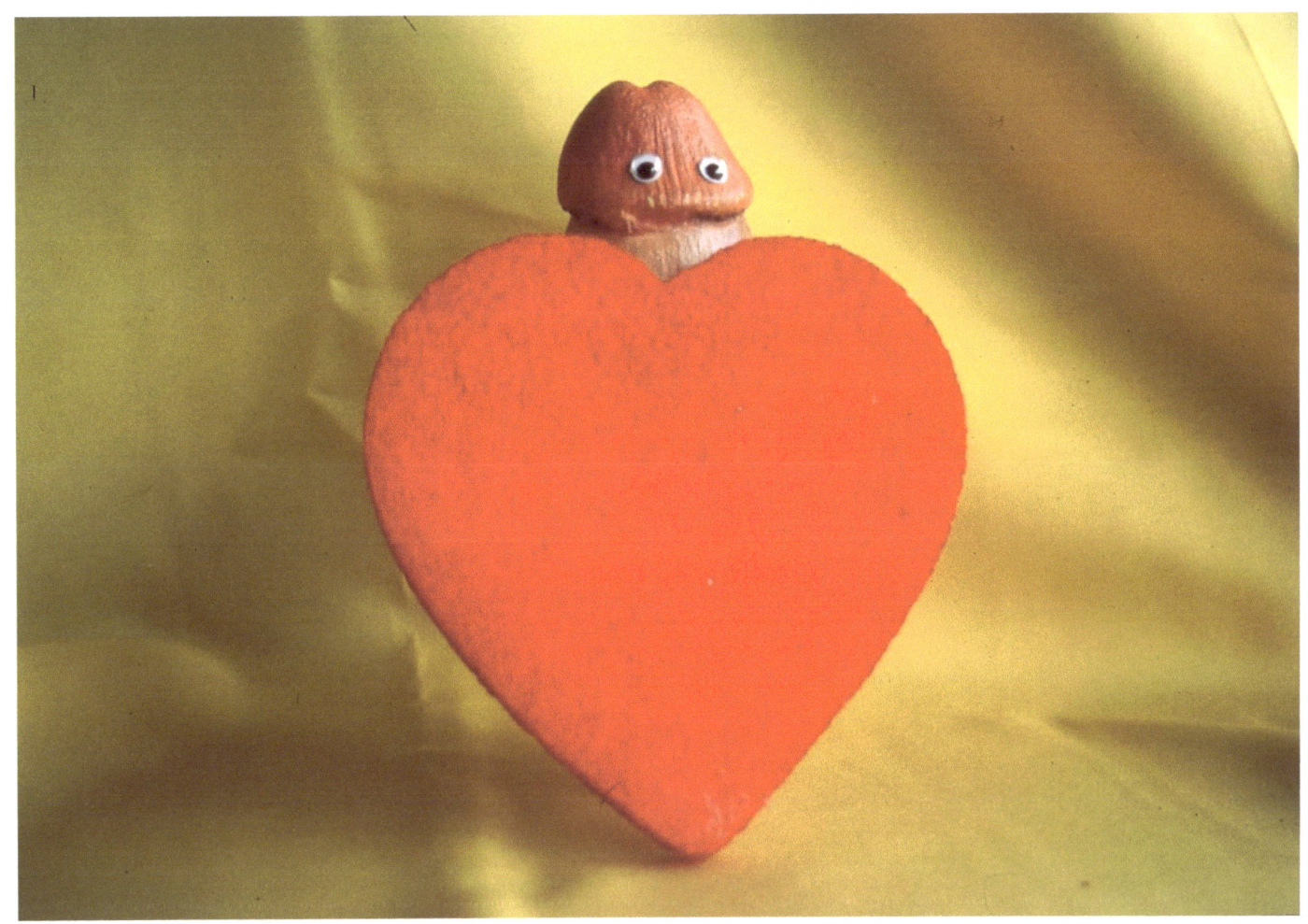

HEART ON FOR YOU

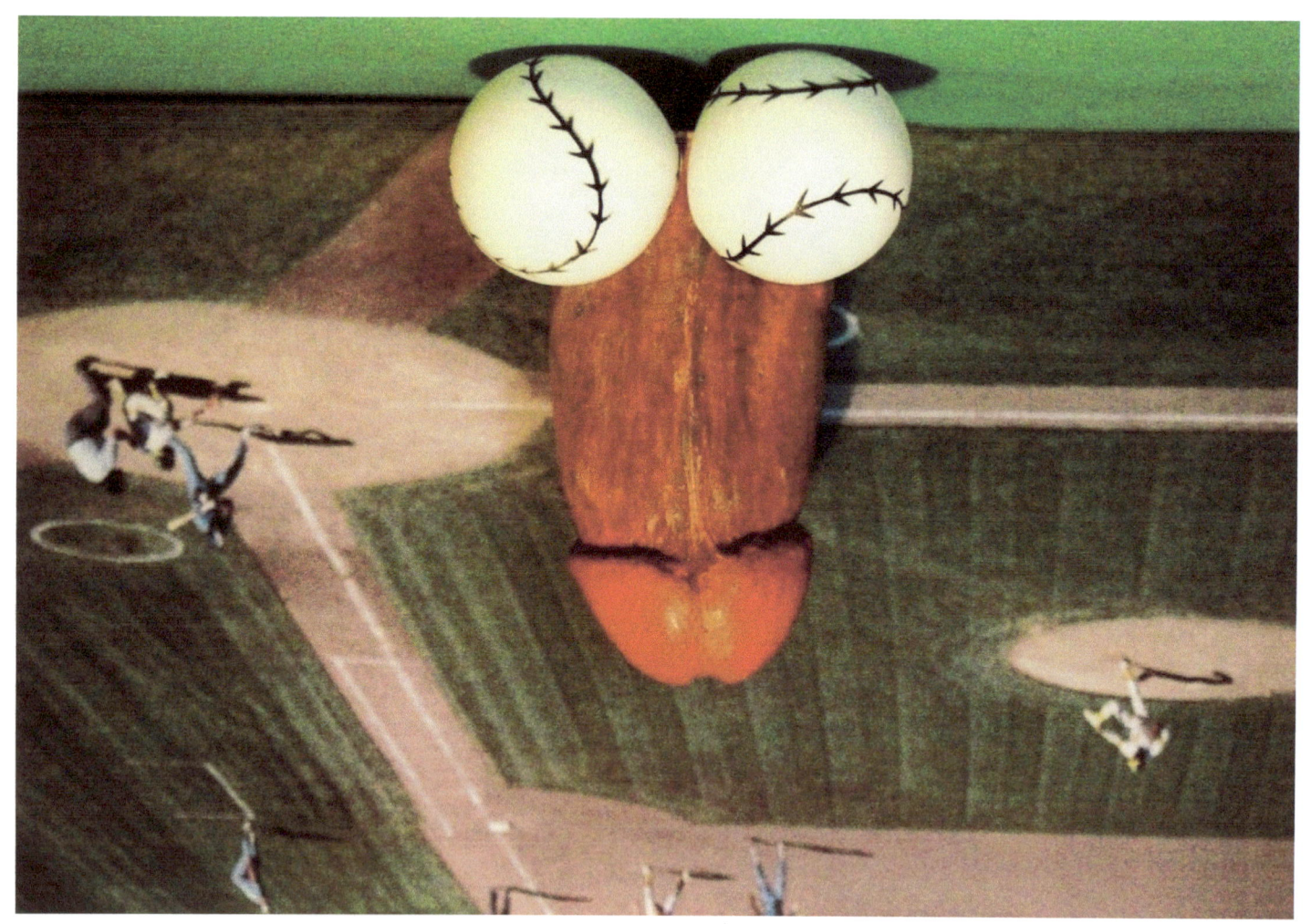

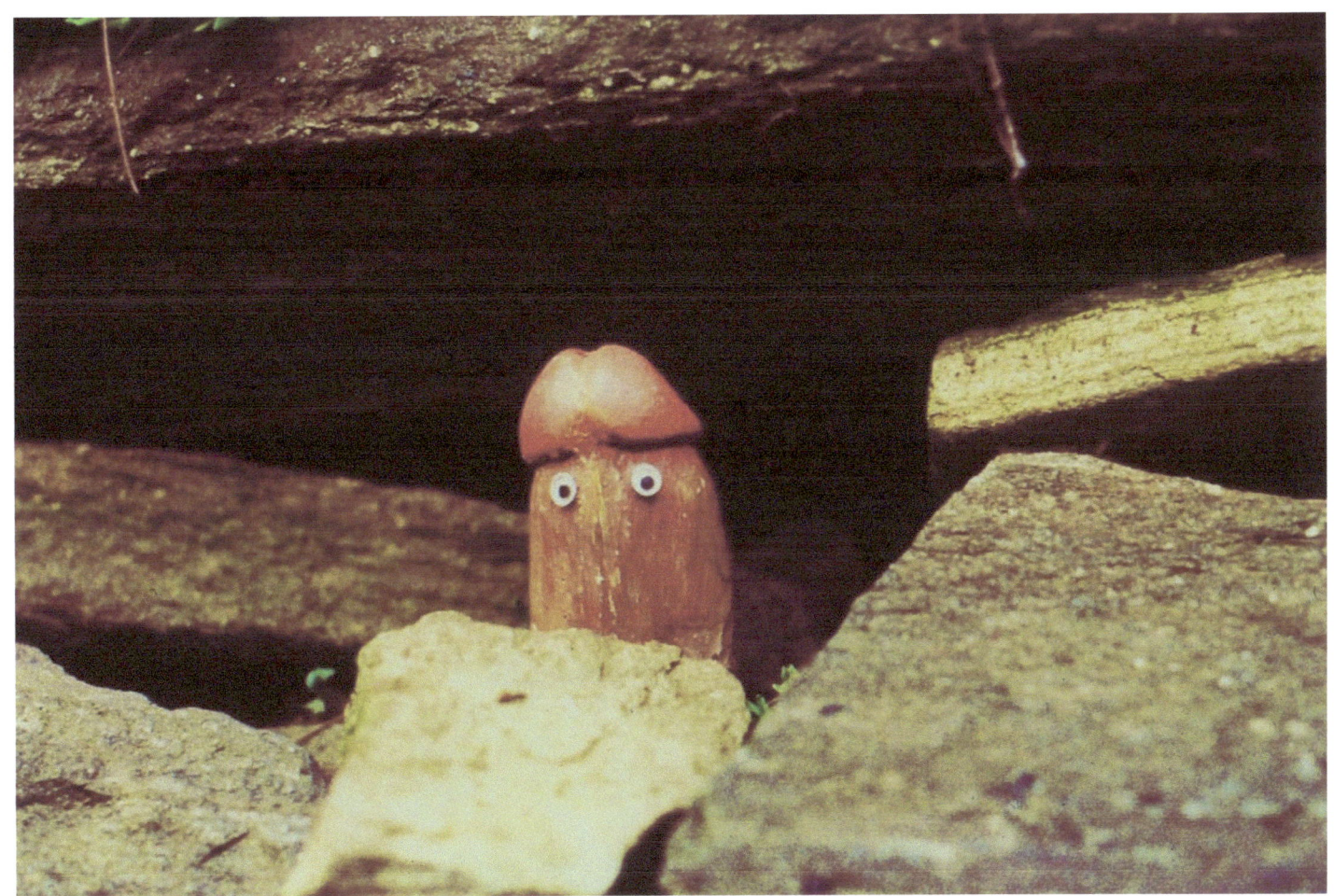

CAVEMAN

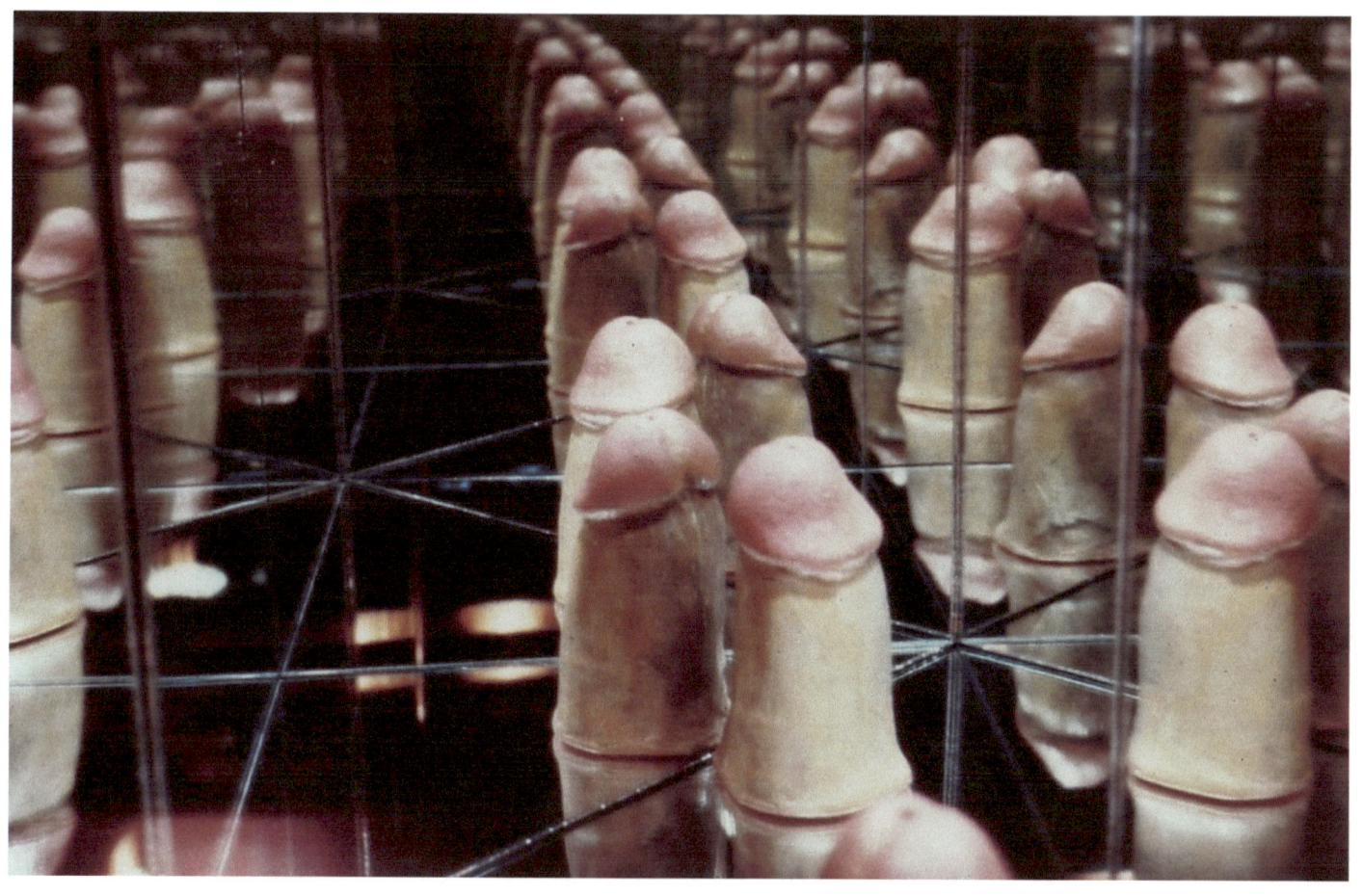

PARADE OF THE WOODY SOLDIERS

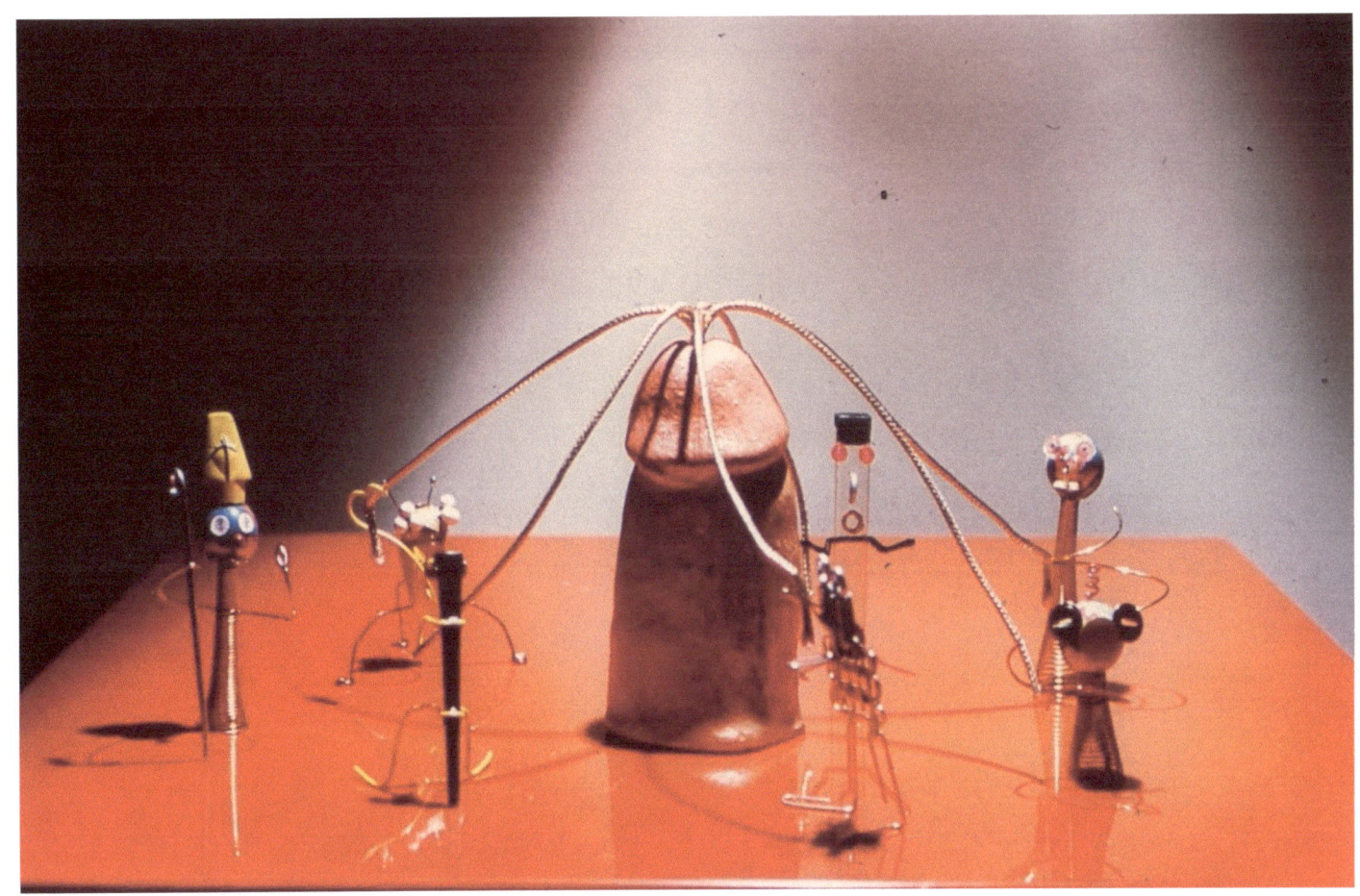

INTERGALACTIC MAYPOLE DANCE

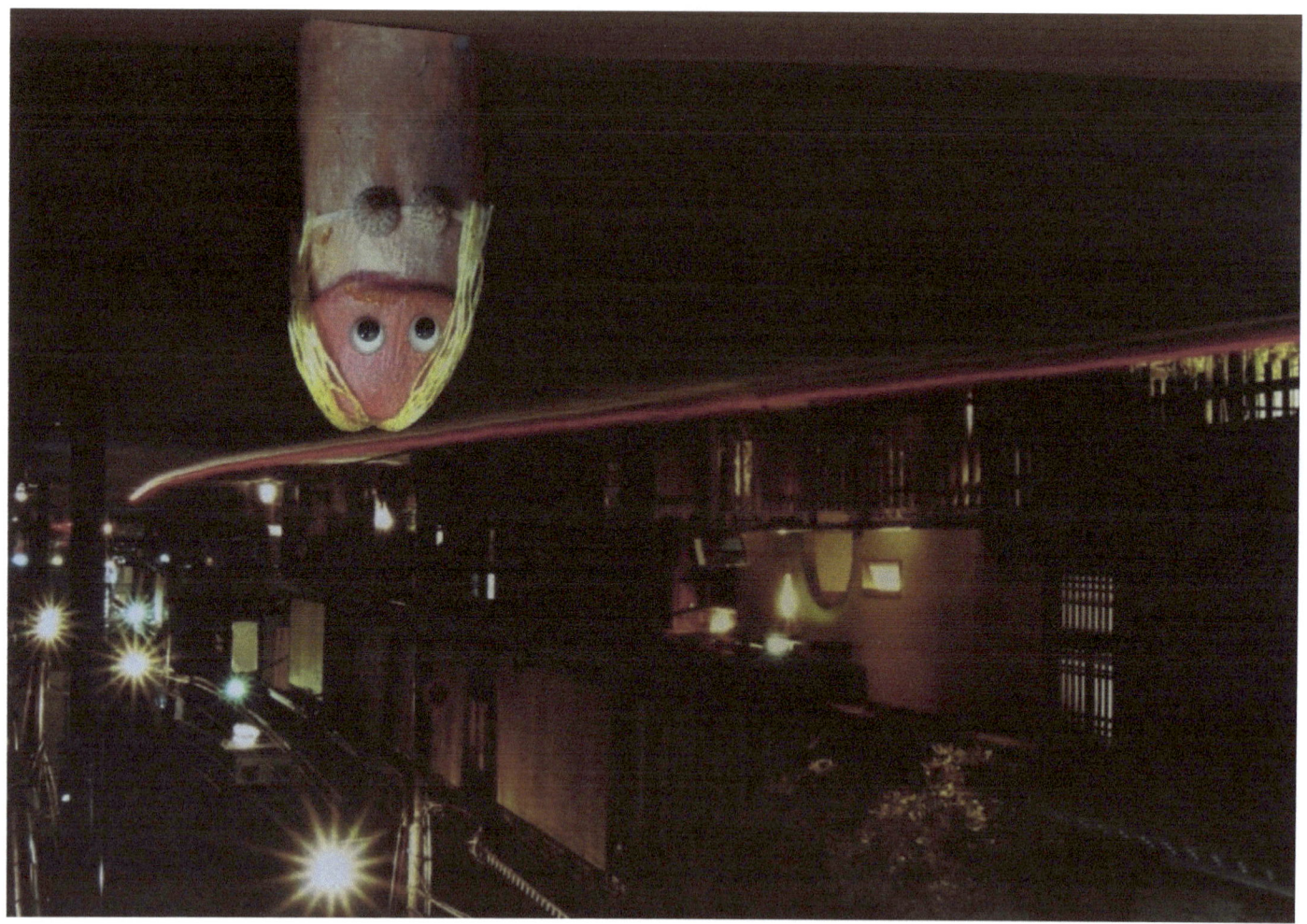

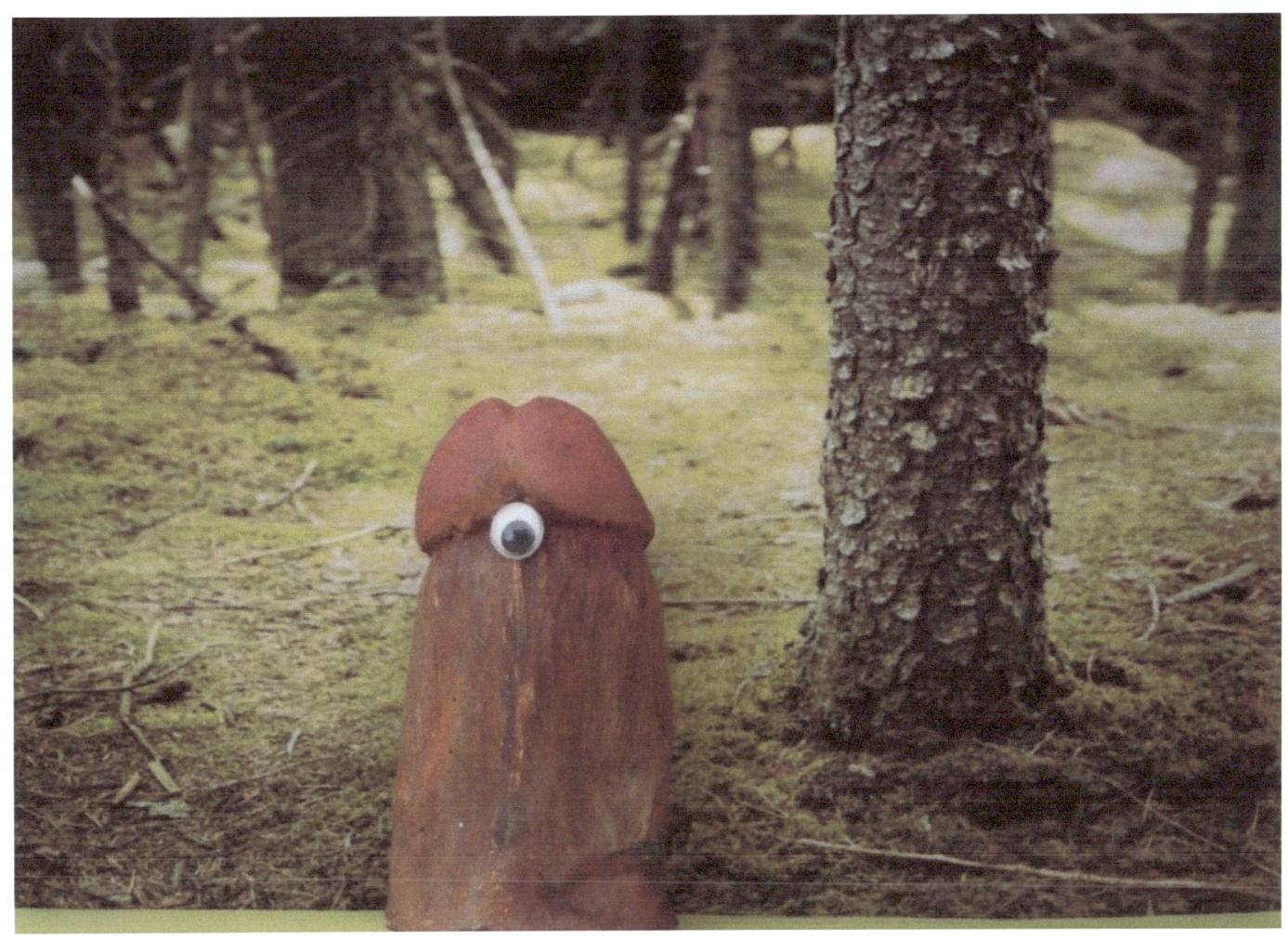

CYCLOPS

RIDE 'EM COWBOY

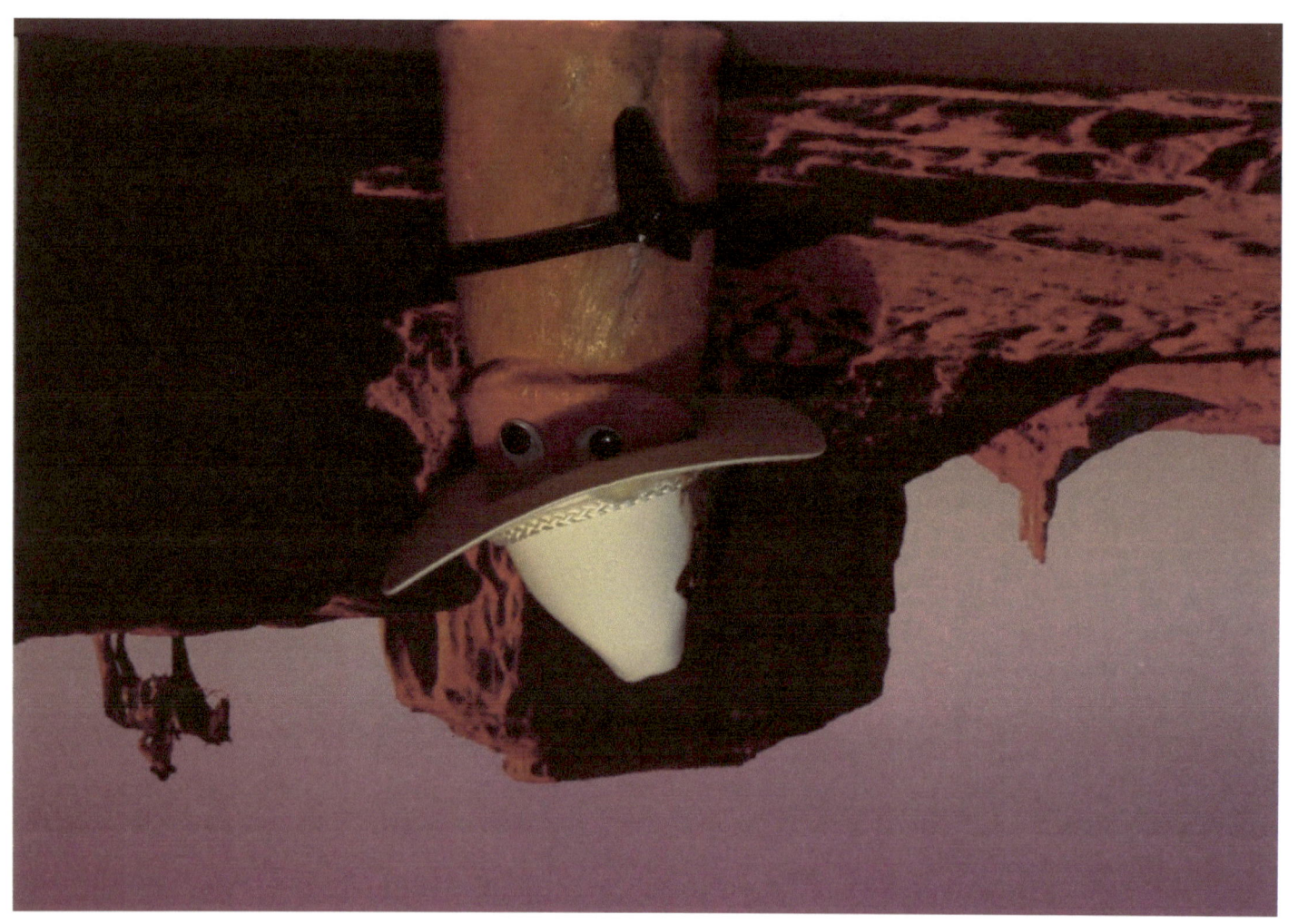

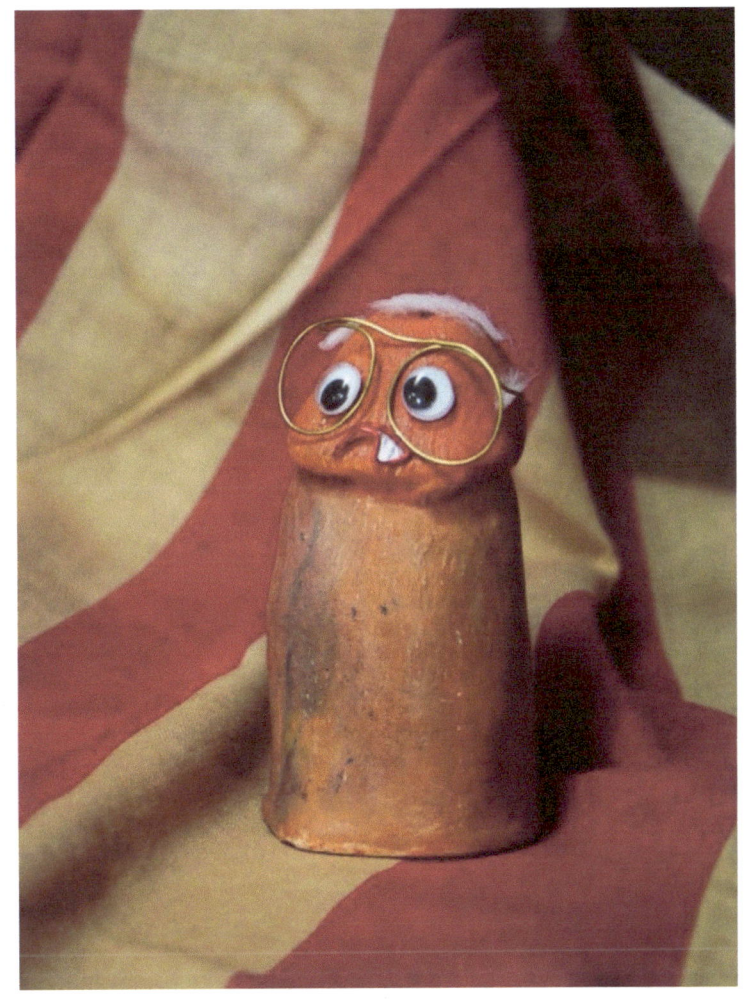

DICK C

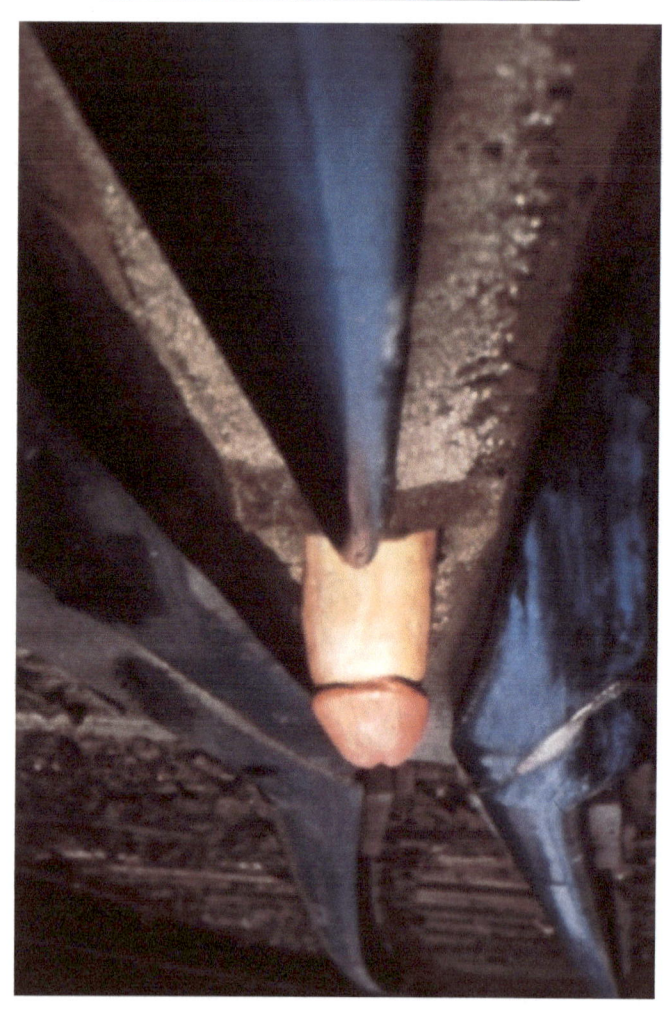

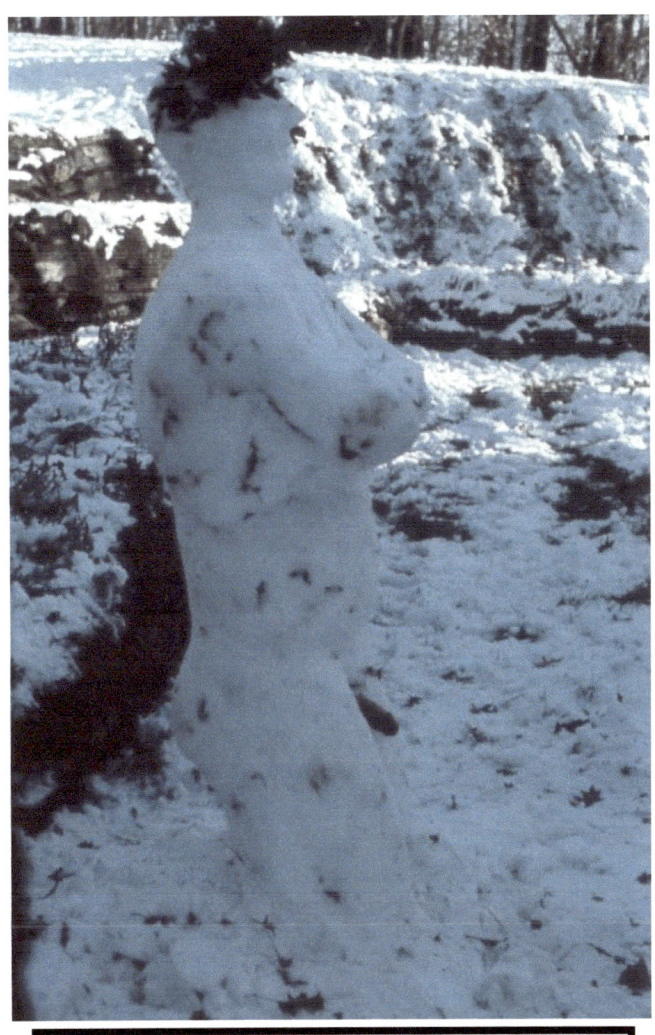

THE ICEMAN COMETH

The Odd Couple—Peter & Spike

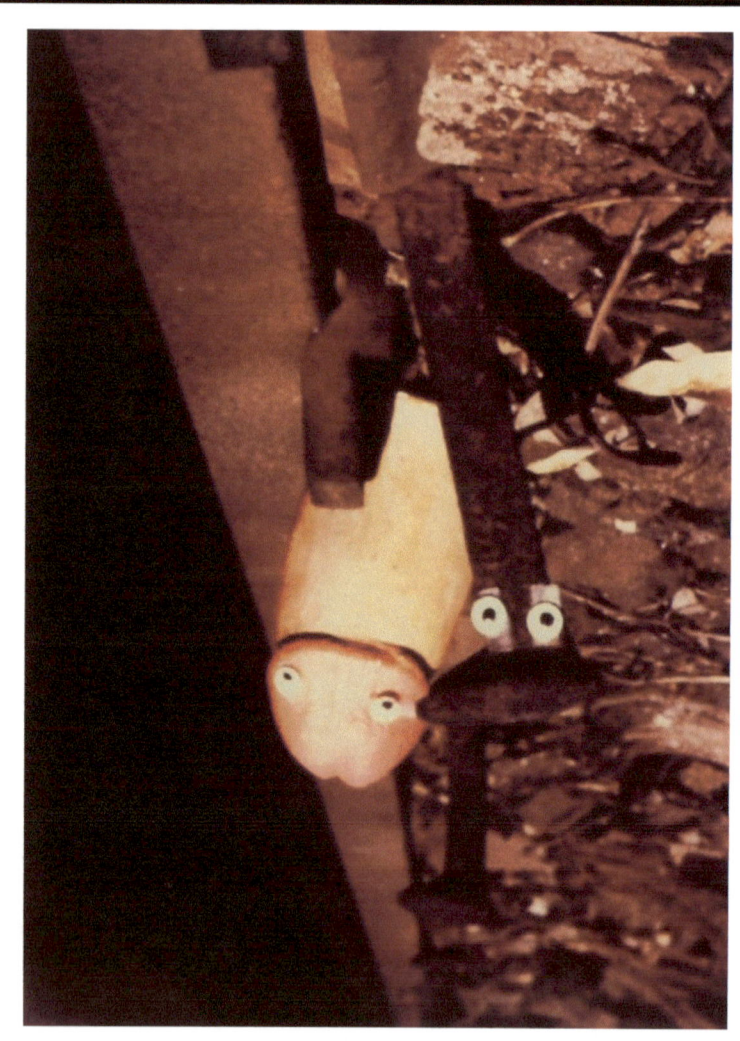

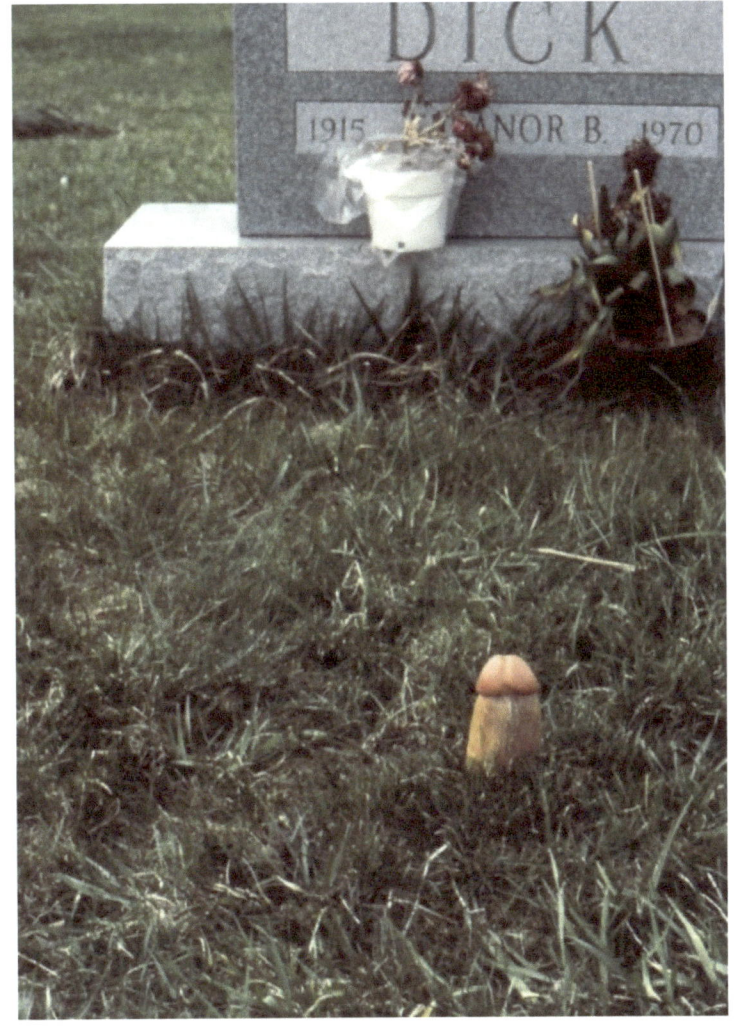

LIFE AFTER DEATH

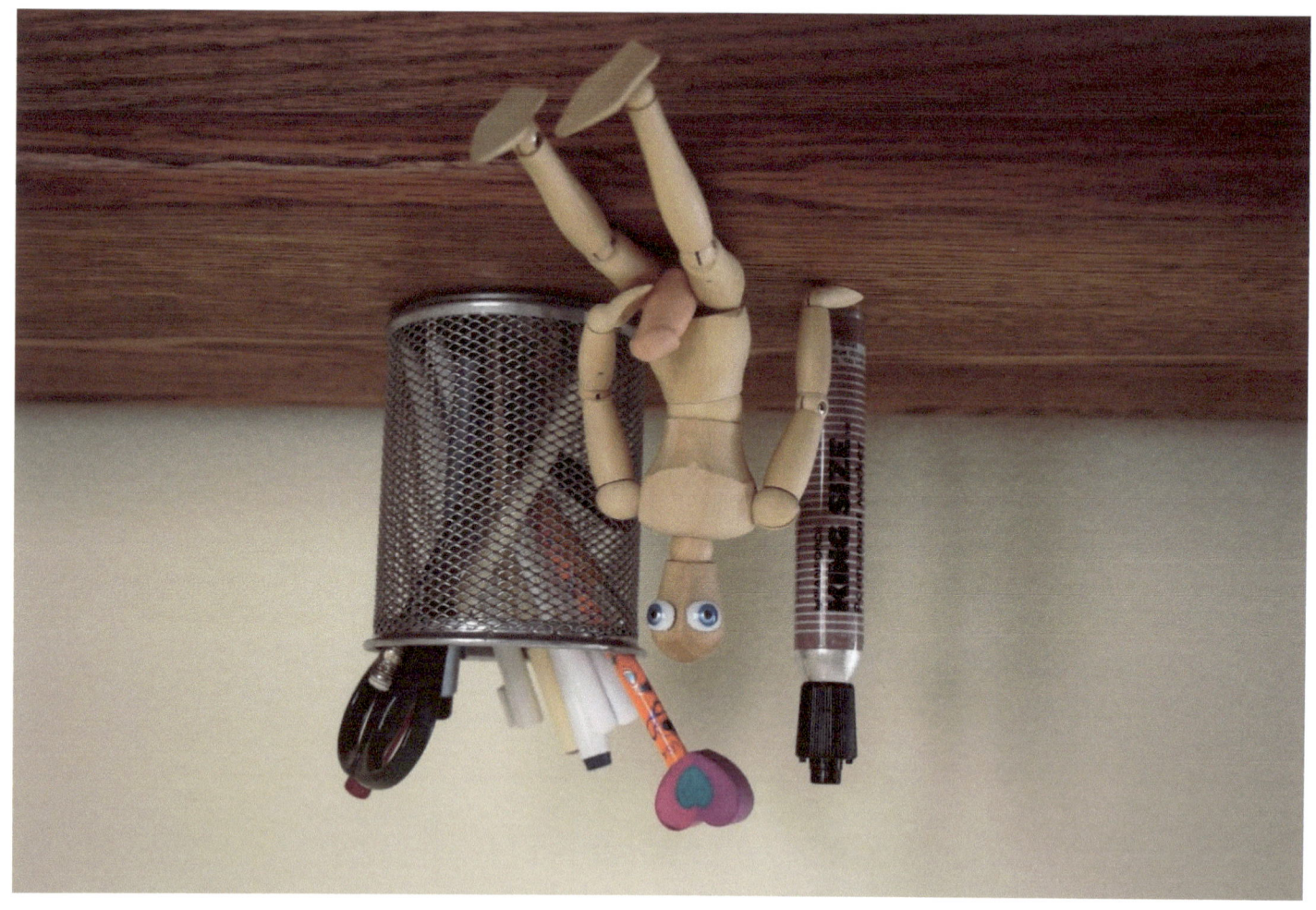

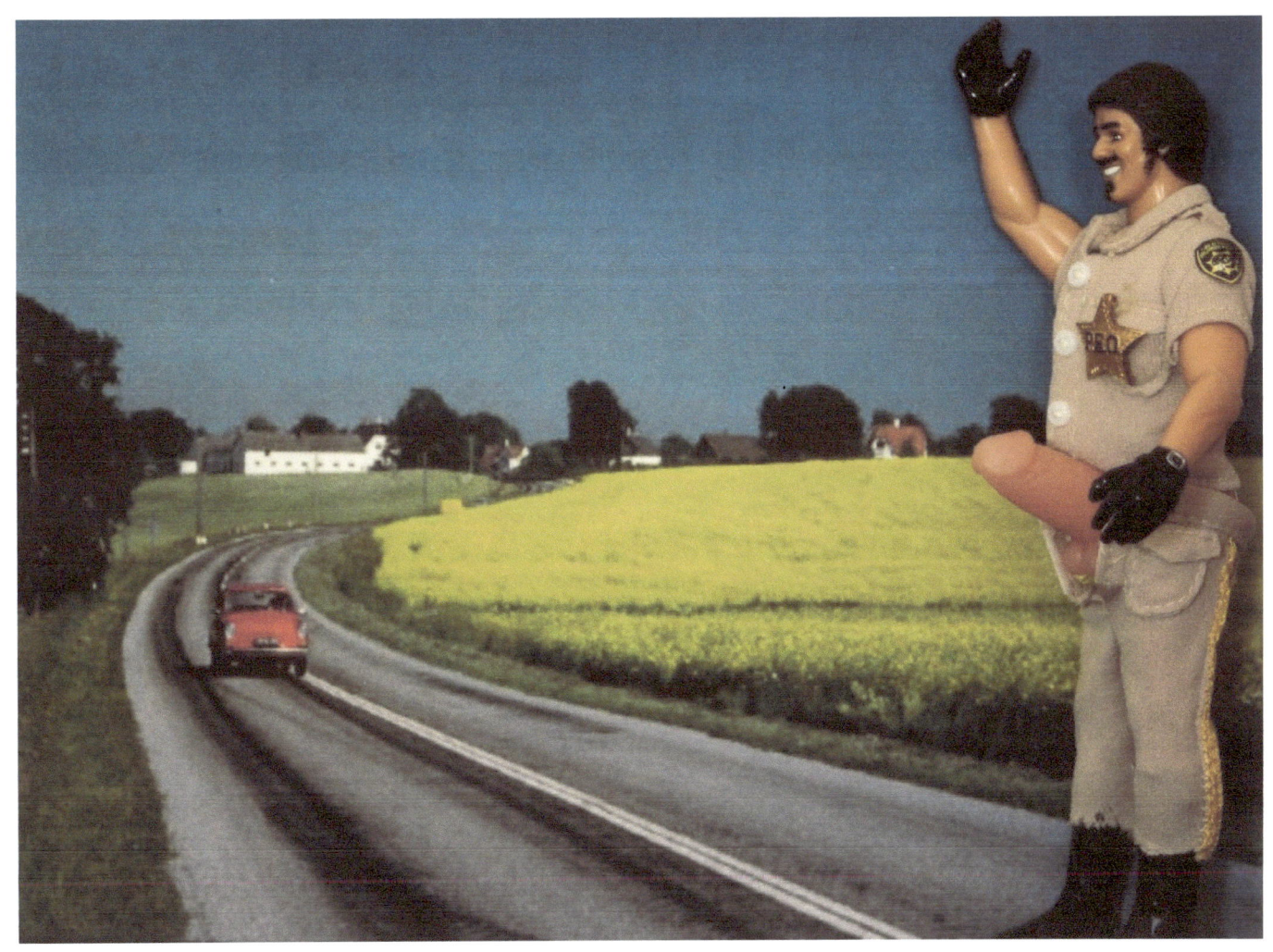

OFFICER FRIENDLY

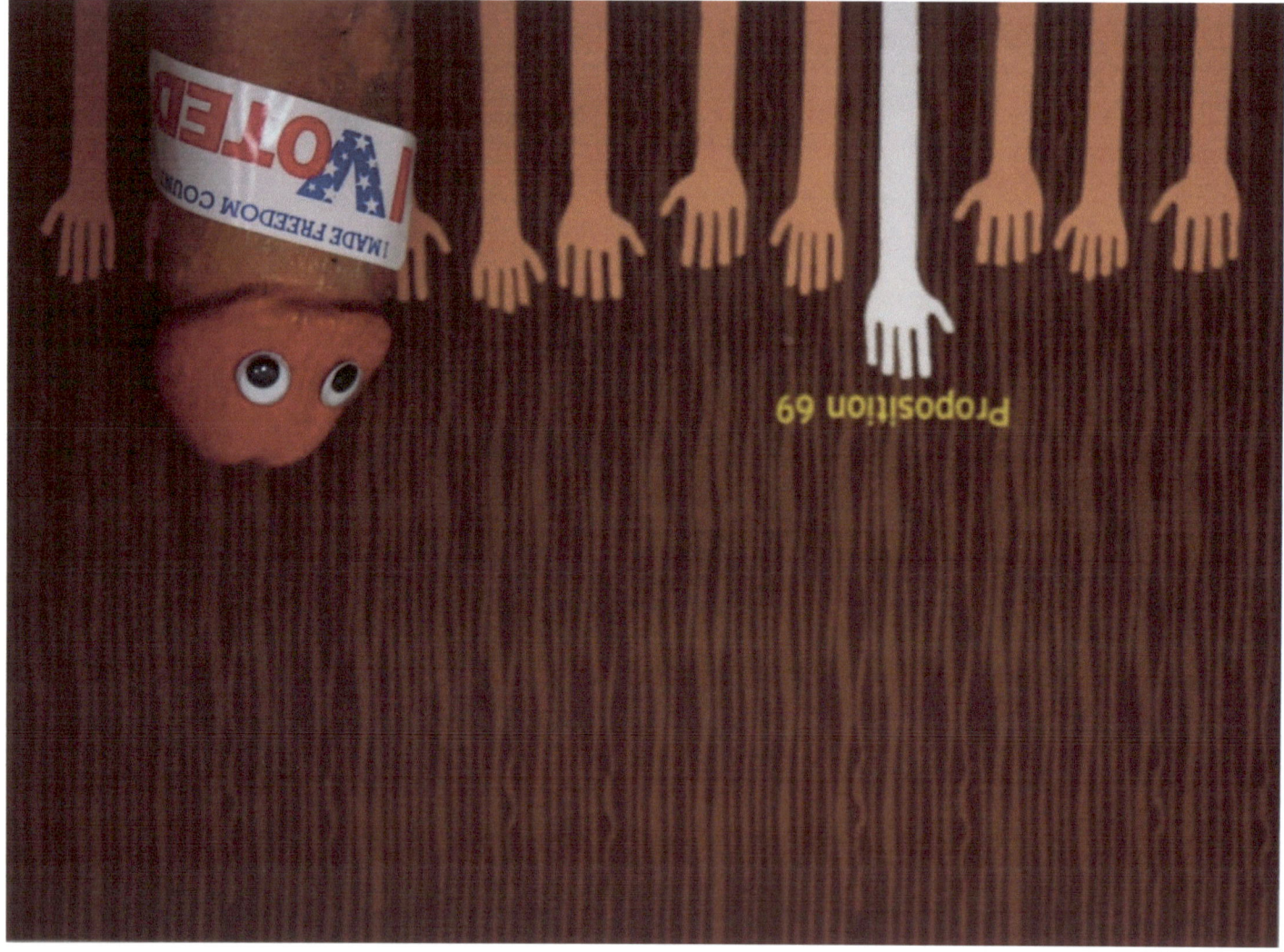

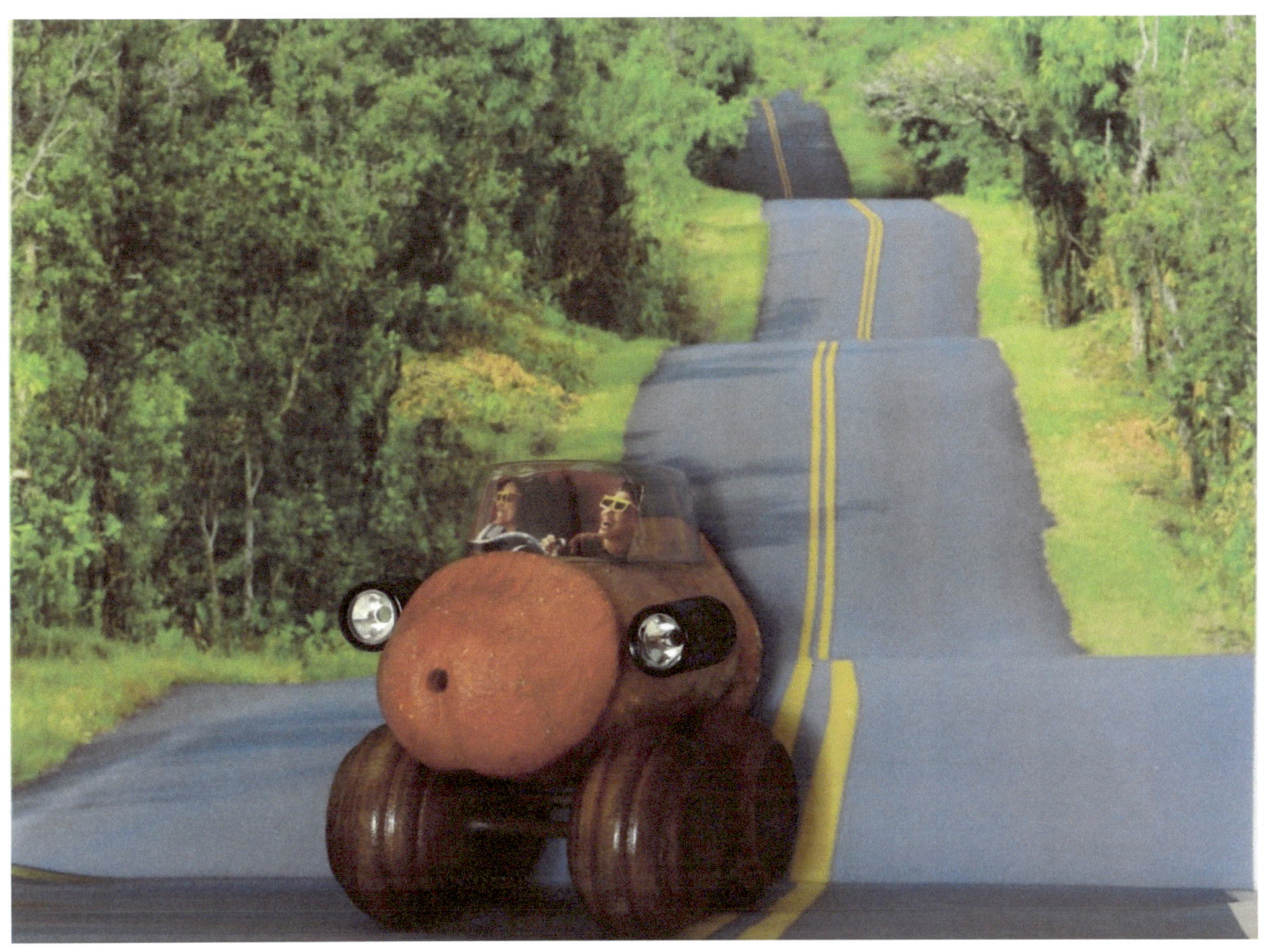

HOT ROD

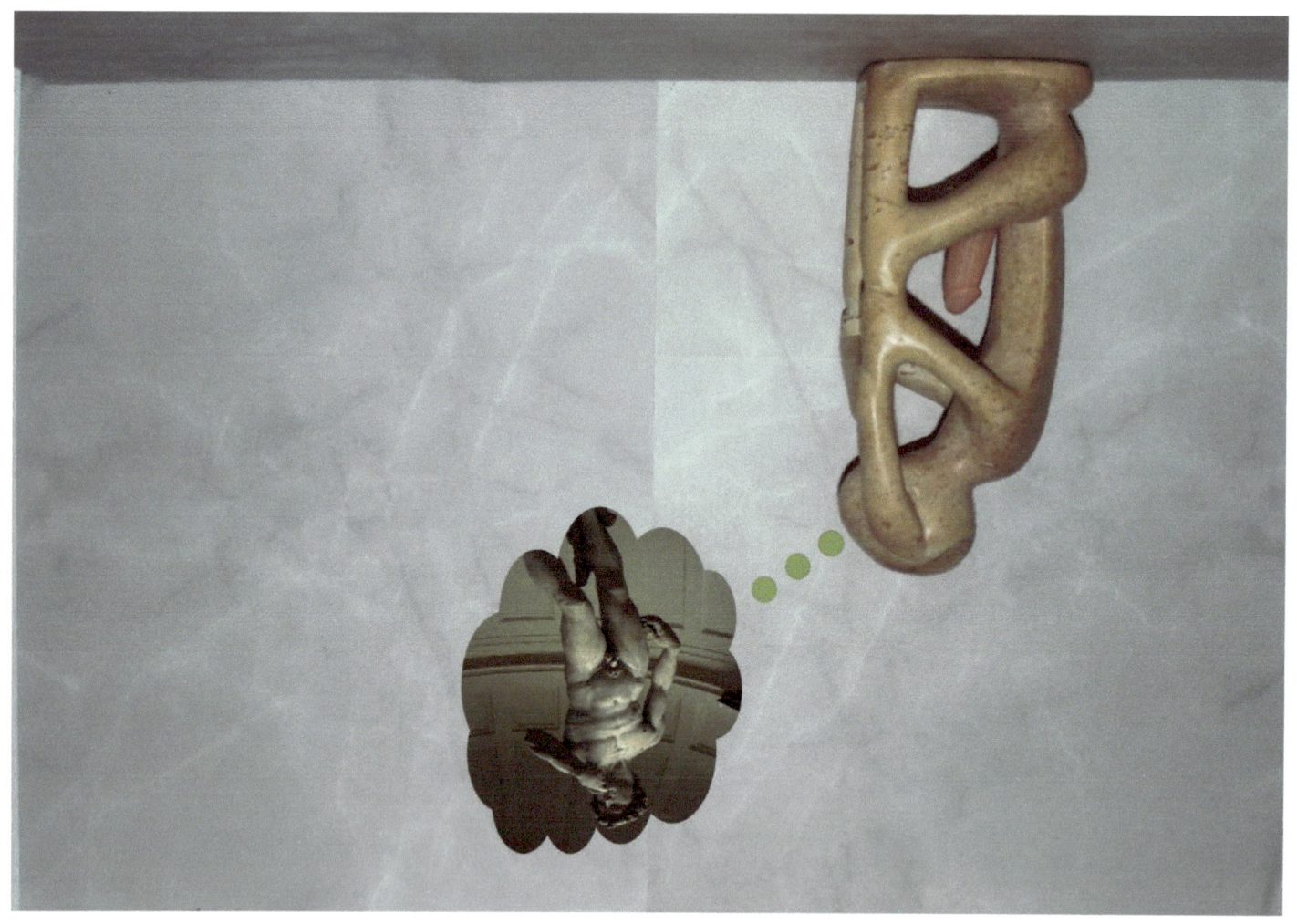

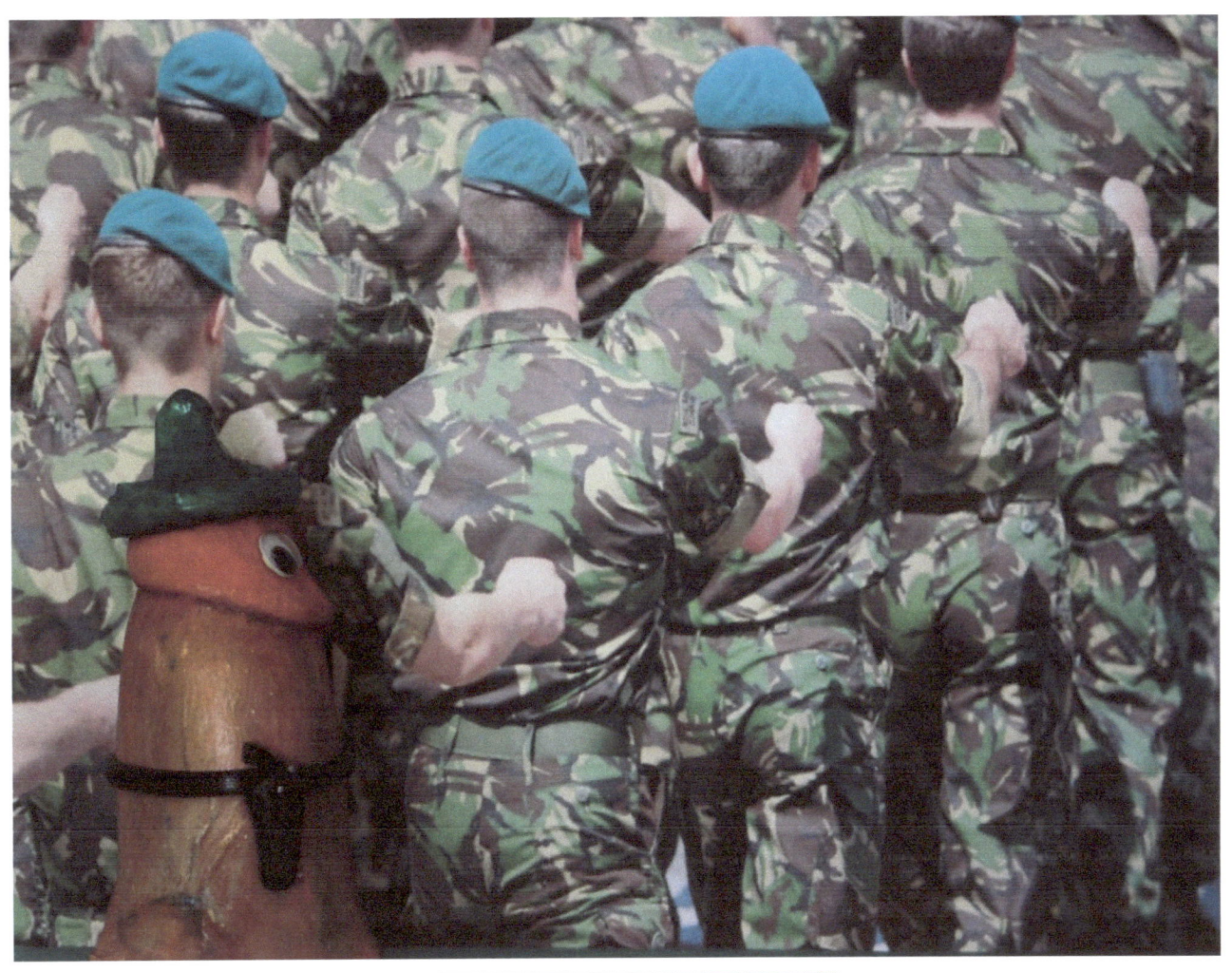

GREEN BERET

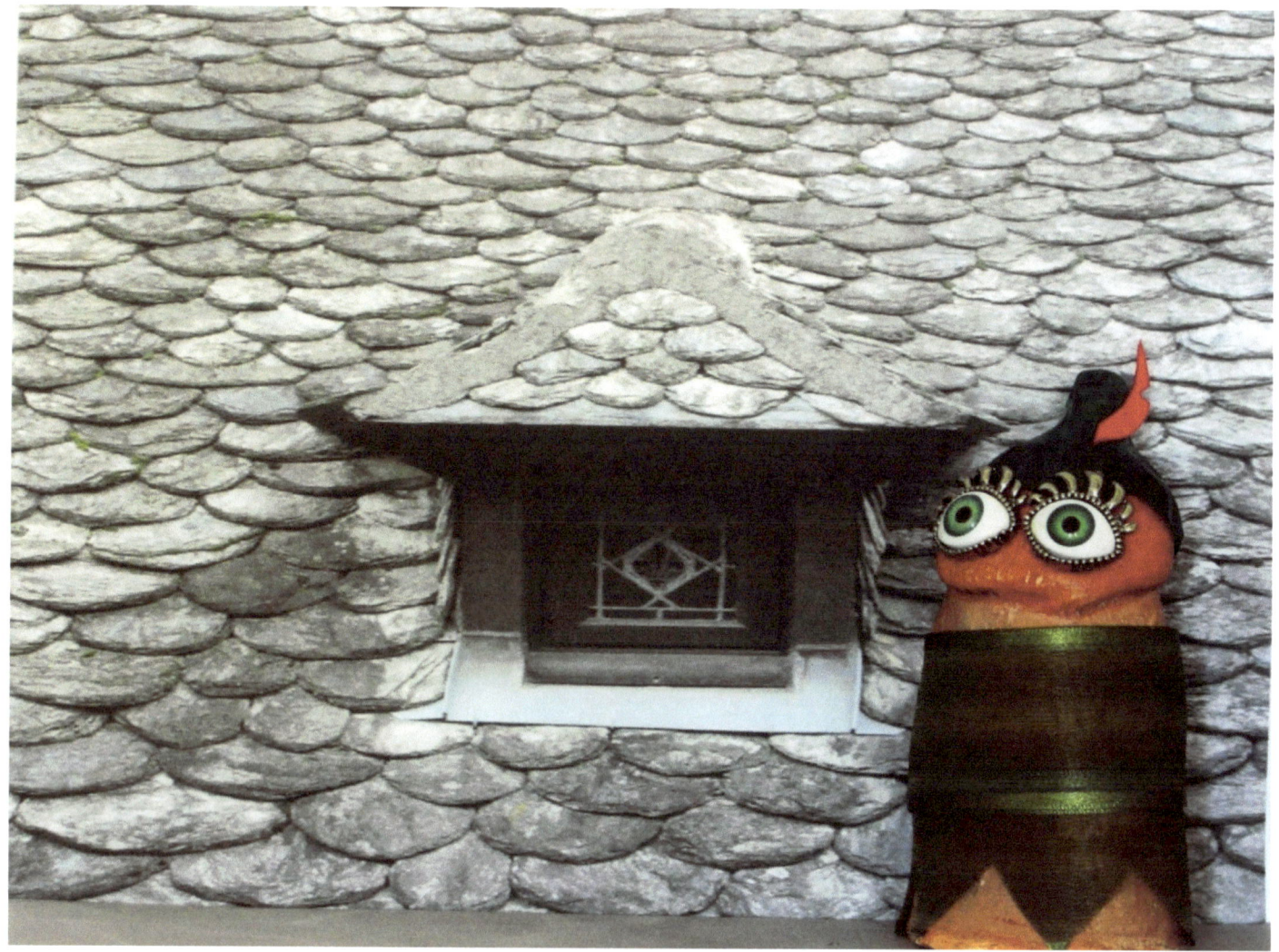

PETER PANSY

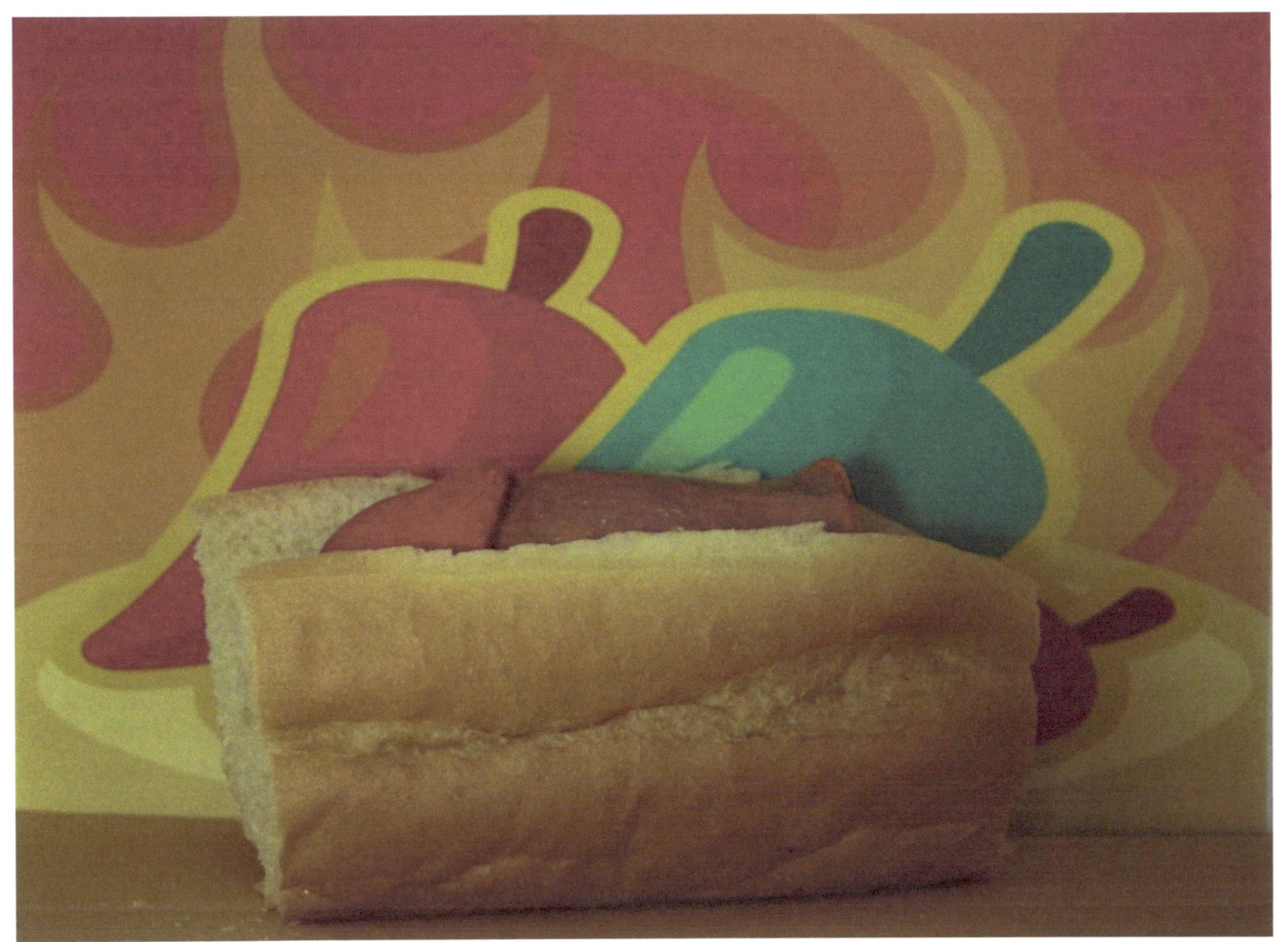

WIENER

O'LAY SEÑORITA

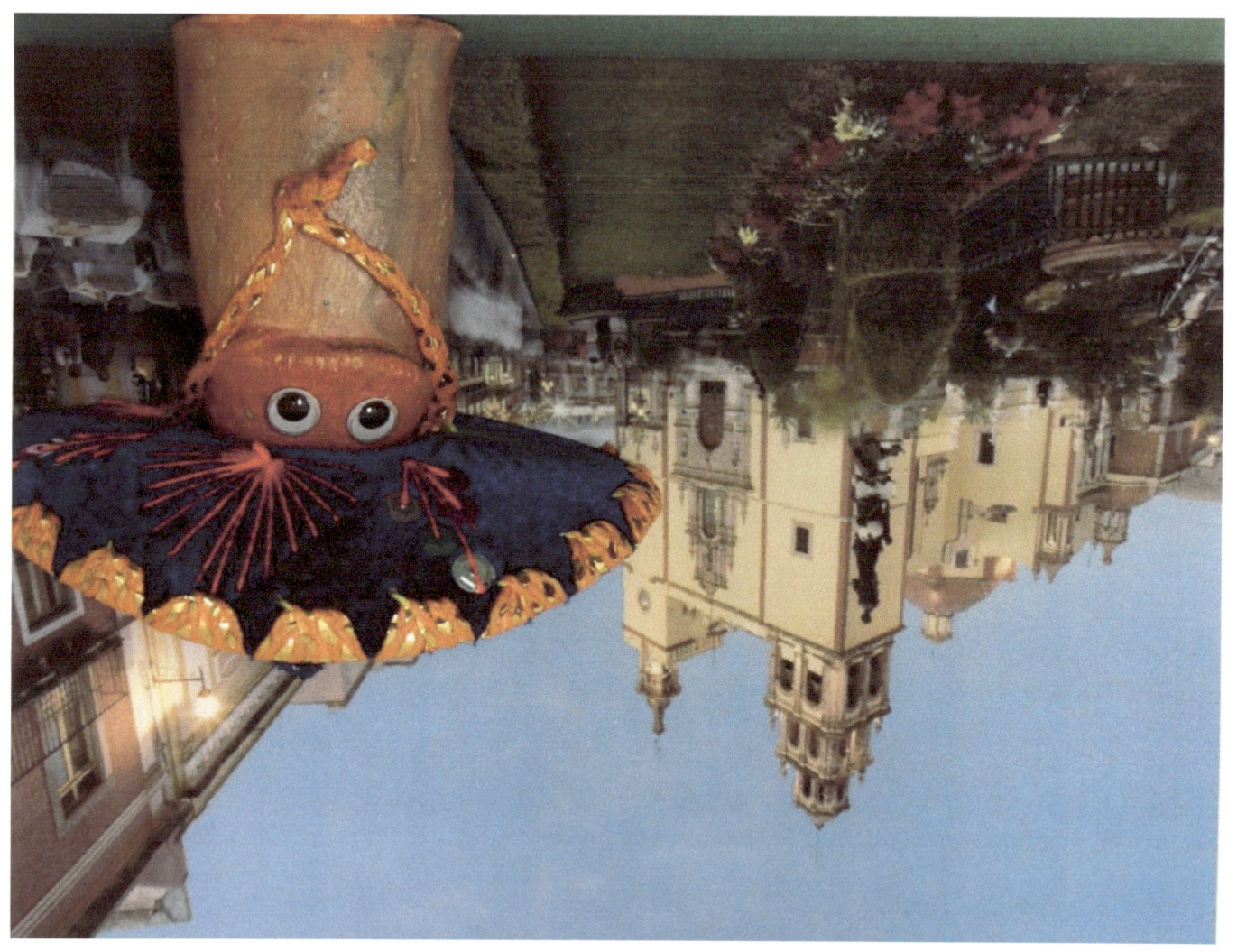

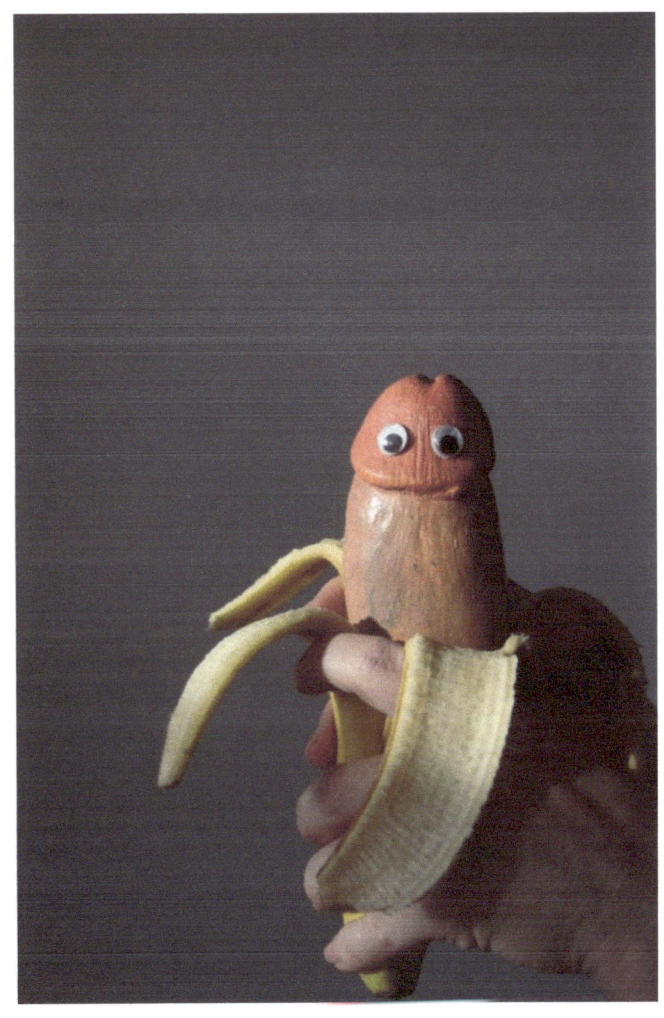

DICKITA BANANA

CROCODILE

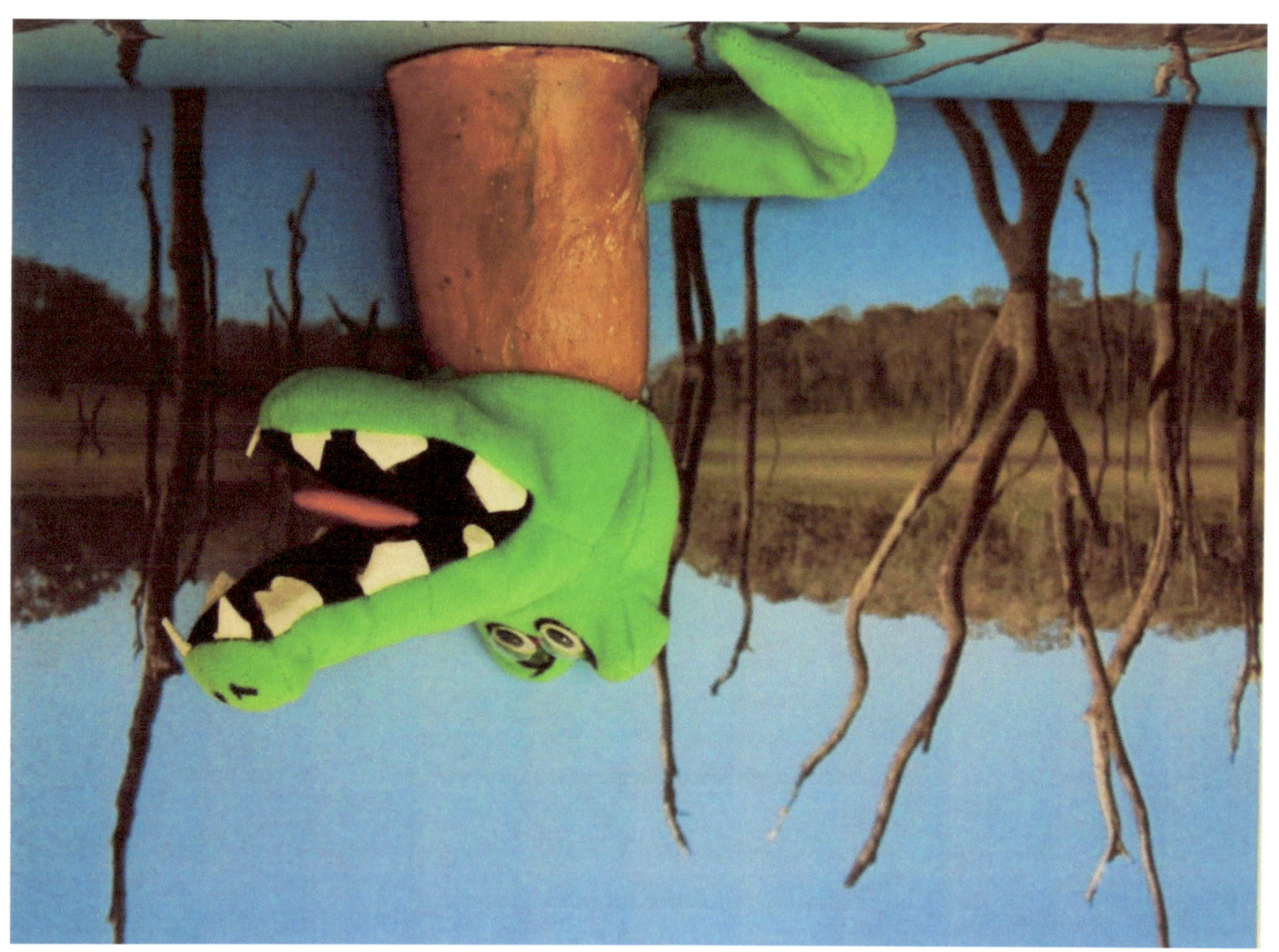

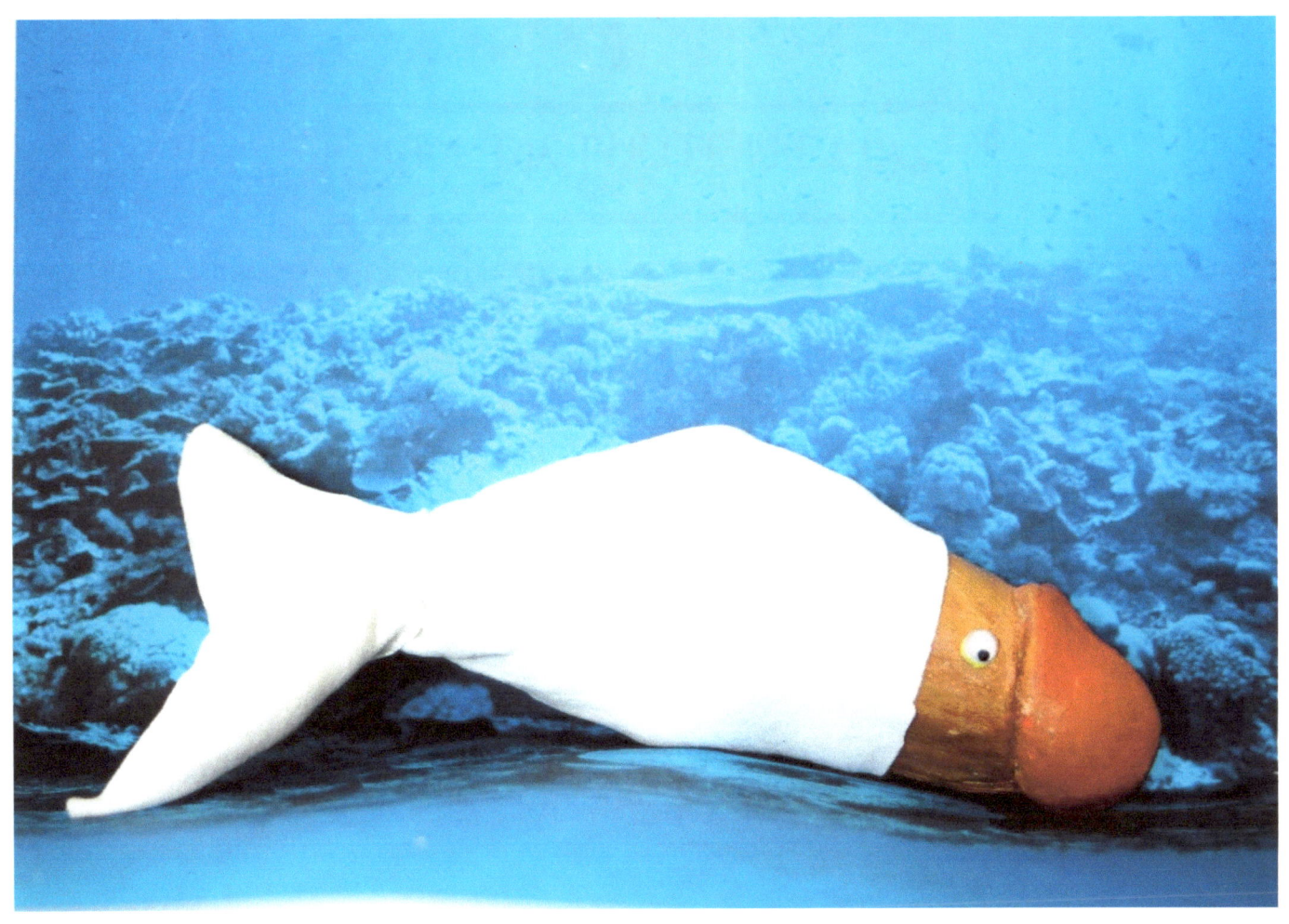

MOBY DICK

RIDE MY LITTLE PRETTY?

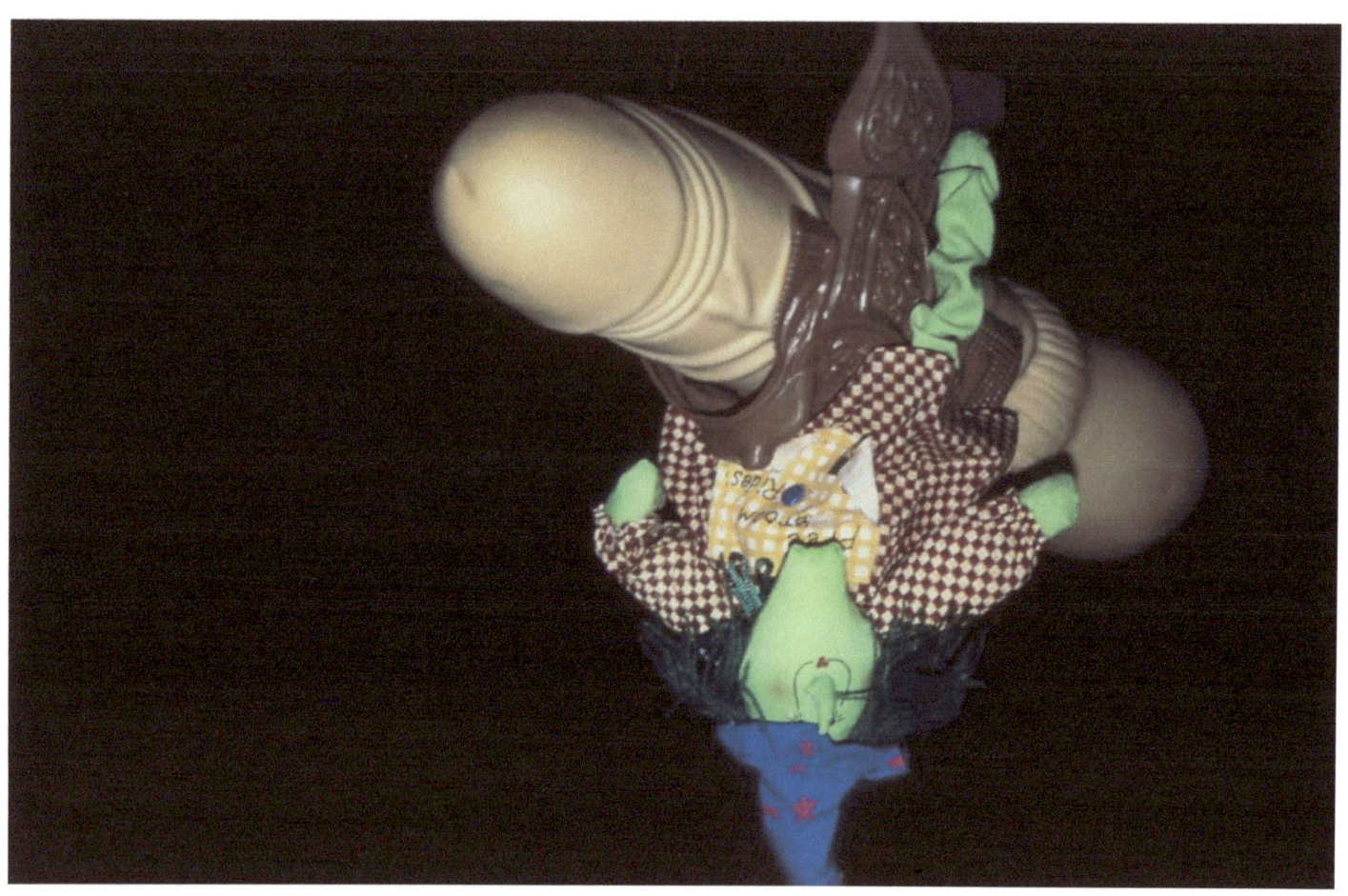

www.ingramcontent.com/pod-product-compliance
Lightning Source LLC
Chambersburg PA
CBHW050756180526
45159CB00003B/1476

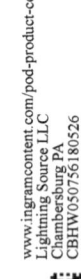